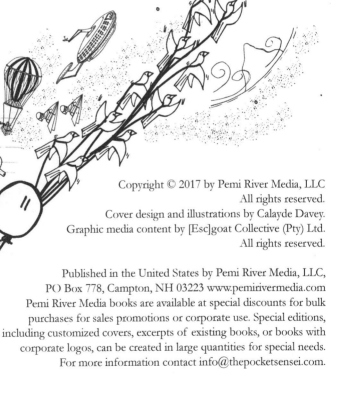

Published in the United States by Pemi River Media, LLC,
PO Box 778, Campton, NH 03223 www.pemirivermedia.com
Pemi River Media books are available at special discounts for bulk
purchases for sales promotions or corporate use. Special editions,
including customized covers, excerpts of existing books, or books with
corporate logos, can be created in large quantities for special needs.
For more information contact info@thepocketsensei.com.

ISBN-13: 978-1975601300
ISBN-10: 1975601300

"*The Pocket Sensei* is beautiful — filled with dynamic illustrations that will help every aspiring and experienced Lean leader study, relish, and apply the advice from two geniuses: Taiichi Ohno and Dr. Shigeo Shingo. *The Pocket Sensei* is wonderful — it will become a best seller."

— Norman Bodek
President of PCS Press and godfather of Lean

"Hal Macomber & Calayde Davey open a new path, taking a different route, and establishing a step—by—step principle—based practice. You will change what and how you remember things as you apply more carefully those acts of memory, mastery, and the efforts of your imagination."

— Gregory A. Howell, P.E.
Cofounder and past President of the Lean Construction Institute

"I love *The Pocket Sensei* and intend to use it with DPR project teams as the next level of Lean leadership training. Why? Because Lean leadership is the biggest need and challenge for any enterprise or individual wanting to provide much greater value to their customers. The drawings are a delight and make this book a fun and easy read. Teaching through practice — *kata* — really is the only path to mastery, and this is done very well. I felt as if I were walking in the shoes of the great Lean masters. *The Pocket Sensei* is truly a gift to the world."

— Dean Reed
Advocate, organizer, and educator for Lean and Integrated Project Delivery,
DPR Construction

"*The Pocket Sensei* offers the serious practitioner an opportunity to experience the deeply grounded principles of innovators Ohno and Shingo. When following and reflecting on the 40 *katas*, you prepare yourself and others for the challenging work in your industry, which desperately needs leadership. *The Pocket Sensei* offers something distinctive and good: a serious opportunity to build a working community that supports and grows each other through an optimistic and continuous search for improvement.

— Chauncey Bell
Chairman and Chief of Design at Harvester & Co.

"I see a joyful sharing of how individual managers can learn to lead others through experimentation, to gain knowledge, and improve their work along with the work of others — while having fun!"

— **Pat Boutier**
"The Seven Kata; Toyota Kata, TWI & Lean Training"
Shingo Research & Professional Publication Recipient, 2013.

"Incorporating Lean into my life has had a profound effect on me. It is the best thing that I could have done for my personal and professional career. My work is fulfilling, and I no longer look to my future career with trepidation. Changing a work culture is not easy, and it is filled with calculated failures, but the reward is worth it. I look forward to using this book personally and with teams moving forward. *The Pocket Sensei* provides to us all the opportunity to become our own Lean masters."

— **Brent Nikolin**
Principle Project Manager, Walt Disney Imagineers

"This book is a strong addition to the Lean literature, describing lessons from decades of consulting experience and effective implementation. Of real importance, the authors teach us to pay attention to our mood, the tenor of one's feelings — an essential component in any change environment, yet seldom discussed."

— **Joe Ely**
Vice President—Operations. Cook Biotech Inc.

"While *The Pocket Sensei* teaches us that the perfect state is unreachable, it also teaches us something else. The perfect state is approachable and should be considered a 'True North' guiding principle by Lean teams. In pursuing continuing excellence, a mindset of managing for learning brings about far better results than managing for performance. This is the raison d'être of Lean!"

— **Tariq Abdelhamid**
RHS Chief Lean Performance Officer,
Associate Professor of Lean Construction, Michigan State University

"*The Pocket Sensei* allows us to learn a Lean mindset and teaches us to cultivate our own strengths towards Lean mastery. The book gives us a glimpse into the deep understanding of the processes and people that deliver good work, and more importantly, good relationships. I cannot recommend this body of work enough, and I cannot wait to bring others along and participate in this fresh new optimism of our Lean culture."

— **Josh Levy**
Founder/Owner of Waterstone Properties Group

"One of the main struggles facing people in both the early and advance stages of their Lean journey is how to engage in the practices that bring about change. *The Pocket Sensei's 40 Katas* keep leaders focused on the deliberate practice of fundamental Lean principles. I've found this approach to be extremely helpful in keeping a conscientious focus on continuous Lean practices for my own development, and helping the development of others. Any organization serious about adopting Lean as an operating strategy should be equipping their leaders with *The Pocket Sensei*."

— **Jay Ierardi, PhD, PE**
Partner, AKF Group, LLC

"*The Pocket Sensei* is a standout among the lexicon of Lean literature for its incisive focus on the inner emotional state as a starting point for exploring your individual barriers to the internalization of Lean learning. That focus is also its key innovation: successful Lean transformation must occur internally before you can lead with authenticity or successfully guide your organization in its Lean journey. *The Pocket Sensei* is a must—read for any individual looking to become a Lean leader."

— **Colin Milberg**
Principal at ASKM and Associates

"*The Pocket Sensei* has masterfully distilled decades of mentorship into thoughtful and elegant prose, exercises, and reflections. *The Pocket Sensei* will become a book you can continue to refer back to as you progress on your journey as a lean leader. It is playful yet introspective; both simple and profound.

— **Tom Feliz**
Senior Construction Technology Advisor, Pavia Systems

Hello, Ninja

Welcome to

THE DOJO

This journal belongs to

Dedication

We dedicate this book to supervisors everywhere who understand their job is in service of the people they are supervising. The work is hard. The hours are long. Efforts are often unacknowledged by both those being supervised and the supervisors' managers. Yet, there is hope.

Lean management is sweeping all industries. Lean thinking has the chance to make everyone's job a little easier, a little safer, and a little more interesting each and every day. To succeed, Lean thinking has to show up in the changed actions and behaviors of those who are leading and managing the work — at all organizational levels.

We offer this book to those who are Lean leaders or who aspire to be Lean leaders in their organizations, on their projects, and among their peers. Perhaps it will go a little way towards making the work setting more supportive to supervisors and those being supervised everywhere.

Special Acknowledgment

I never met Taiichi Ohno or Dr. Shigeo Shingo. I first learned about Lean through their books. Of course, I never learned Lean until I had responsibility for the Lean journey in my company. Still, these books played a big part in preparing me for my role.

The English translation of these books are Norman Bodek's legacy. Norman also built a publishing company, Productivity Press, that was eventually responsible for translating and publishing over a hundred Japanese-language books. To this day, there is no greater collection of Lean thinking than the Productivity Press collection.

Norman didn't know anything about manufacturing when he decided to translate and publish the books. He had a hunch. Unlike others, he acted on a hunch. Here we are today! Hundreds of books later, the world has the knowledge of the Lean masters to guide their way. It is fair to say that Norman is the godfather of Lean management.

It all started in 1981 with Shigeo Shingo's book *A Study of the Toyota Production System from an Industrial Engineering Perspective*, which came to be known as the "green book." Norman found the book in Japan, ordered 500 copies in English, and went on to sell 35,000 copies to readers of his Productivity Newsletter. While the original translation was tough to read, for those of us who were industrial engineers, the content was fascinating. Dr. Shingo shared a refreshing way of how he thought about production system design.

The book was successful enough that Norman published four other Shingo titles at Productivity Press, and an easier-to-read re-translation of the green book. Along the way, Norman also published three books by Taiichi Ohno. The first two, *Toyota Production System* and *Workplace Management*, augmented the Shingo canon. With the third Ohno book, *Just in Time for Today and Tomorrow*, Productivity Press also rediscovered Henry Ford's classic *Today and Tomorrow*, a book which had been long out of print. After a long investigation, Norman eventually found a copy of Ford's' book at a Connecticut Library — and it happened to be available in Japanese as well! Norman acquired the rights to the book, and it is now available on Amazon.

As of June 2017, Norman has made 88 study missions and visits to Japan. Each time he comes back enthused by what he learned. Recently, he told me of the "geniuses" he met and what we can learn from them. When Norman calls someone a genius he is not being generous. Norman has a knack for identifying the best thinking in the world and he puts his money where his mouth is — he publishes the genius's work. Norman recently published Shigeo Shingo's *Fundamental Principles of Lean Manufacturing* and *Kaizen and the Art of Creative Thinking*, two books that were sitting on Mrs. Shingo's shelf. Norman was also instrumental in setting up the "Shingo Prize for Operational Excellence" at the University of Utah, the same institution that awarded Shingo an honorary Ph.D.

In a recent conversation with Norman, he offered me insights on what made Engineer Ohno and Dr. Shingo stand as masters among many experts. Ohno insisted people go to the source to see for themselves — *genchi genbutsu* — and to challenge the status quo. Shingo, Norman says, would ask anyone performing an operation what the value-adding ratio was and then how they would improve it. You'll see those behaviors (among others) discussed throughout the lessons in this book.

In the last few years Norman discovered Takashi Harada, a former high school coach, who created a system for developing people called the *Harada Method*. Norman learned this method himself, and developed it into a teaching and certification system applicable to a number of industries.

Norman and his partner Enna continue to publish wonderful titles with PCS Press to this day. Thank you, Norman, for providing the rich material from which I created this small book. I just hope I have done justice to the Lean masters Norman introduced to the world.

— Hal Macomber

Forward

WHAT IS THIS LITTLE BOOK?

The Pocket Sensei offers something distinctive and good: a platform for learning to make improvements in many industries. The heroes of the book, Taiichi Ohno and Shigeo Shingo, were the hard-thinking and hard-working Japanese engineers that led Toyota from the ashes of WWII. Toyota rose in the following decades to its unprecedented dominance over the great automotive companies of the United States, the United Kingdom, and Germany.

What Hal Macomber and Calayde Davey have delivered here is an easily accessible foundational introduction to what these remarkable engineers built for themselves and upon which they built the Toyota Production System. Hal and his former partner Gregory Howell have long been among the most serious students of Ohno and Shingo. What Toyota learned and invented has had far-reaching positive effects in manufacturing and many other industries. Not since Henry Ford's original orchestration of vertically integrated mass production have we seen anywhere near as influential an impact on industrial work as what Toyota did.

The Pocket Sensei stands in front of doors behind which are found many failed initiatives, Lean and otherwise, across many industries. How many times have we seen massive rework in architectural, engineering, or marketing communication? How many software companies are underestimating or overestimating their market needs, unable to catch critical errors quickly enough, redoing work or misplacing the efforts of their labor to customers' real expectations and value? Lean practices found their way to hospital settings by improving patient outcomes, yet how many nurses face routine inconsistencies and are frustrated in their attempts to bring improvements to enable critical changes? How many people struggle to work through their observations with their teams, or share their sensibilities across multiple organizations quickly enough to provide services where they are most needed? Who are we serving in our industries, our organizational processes, and the execution of good work?

Construction provides a fine example of failures. The growing critical demand for infrastructure and construction is global, and it is not being met. By almost any measure, construction is one of the saddest industries in the West. Its participants have experienced almost no overall improvements in productivity for more than 50 years. The industry is famous for breeding bad moods, unhappy work environments, and perhaps most notably, mistrust and resentment. A standard practice in the industry is still to 'win' contracts with low bids and then make money from change orders — what is often called, in other environments, 'bait and switch.' In the midst of the massive mistrust that permeates the industry, the predominant 'management strategy' is building many layers of management and supervision that multiply costs, time, errors, frustration, and sap energy and joy from everyone involved. Large projects across asset classes typically take 20 percent longer to finish than scheduled and end up to 80 percent over budget.[1] McKinsey tells us that there is a $1.6 trillion productivity deficit in the construction industry — $1.6 trillion in opportunities in construction alone to improve the way we build our world, just by focusing on productivity improvements.[2] The opportunity is immense. And construction is not the only industry confronting massive process and productivity opportunities. The world needs a change in the way that we work with each other and learn to serve each other better.

Neither this book nor the tradition called Lean will address those opportunities on their own. Revolutionizing industries, transforming any particular company or actor, or even repairing a sizable project underway calls for a great deal more than 40 *katas*. But what *The Pocket Sensei* offers is not from the American tradition of Lean.[3] Most of those who employ this word today think that they are pointing intelligibly to coherent, valuable practices, tools, and methods —whether originally derived from the Toyota experiences or not — that will move people and organizations towards some cohesive path of improved action. However, the word 'Lean' itself does not reliably indicate any particularly organized direction of thinking for improving a difficult situation, despite what we might guess from reflecting on old jargon such as 'lean and mean.' There is no stable method or approach called 'Lean' this or 'Lean' that. Still, Lean has entered the vernacular of many of our worlds in a big way. We have Lean manufacturing, Lean startups, Lean construction, Lean design, and many others. Unfortunately, what the word

---

[1] Agarwal, R., Chandrasekaran, S., & Sridhar, M. (2016, June). *Imagining construction's digital future*. Retrieved from Mickensy Global Institute: http://www.mckinsey.com/industries/capital-projects-and-infrastructure/our-insights/imagining-constructions-digital-future

[2] Barbosa, F., Woetzel, J., Mischke, J., Ribeirinho, M., Sridhar, M., Parsons, M., Brown, S. (2017). *Reinventing Construction: A Route to Higher Productivity*. McKinsey Global Institute.

[3] Used in the way it appears in this book, the term 'Lean' was first coined by John Krafcik in his 1988 article, *Triumph of the Lean Production System*, based on his master's thesis at the MIT Sloan School of Management. Krafcik had been a quality engineer in the Toyota-GM NUMMI joint venture in California before joining MIT for MBA studies. (Thanks, Wikipedia!)

'Lean' points to today is little more than what the word 'modern' indicates.

Those in the West who have attempted to copy Toyota's innovations have universally done so by copying pieces of what the Japanese invented. However, those piecemeal copies are not what the Japanese invented at all. Rather, the original invention was an entirely new cultural style of working. For one piecemeal example, Western businesses picked up a technique that we called 'Just-in-Time' and began re-scheduling the delivery of supplies so they arrived as they were needed in production chains. The practice promised (and often delivered) a nice return on investment. When Western suppliers were not able to deliver on time, businesses replaced them. Just-in-time counted, in the West, as an important innovation all by itself.

However, Western businesses did not see that Toyota had invented an entire and radically new style of coordination with suppliers — a humanistic style that affected every part of the relationship between the companies and people involved. It was centered on a different interpretation about the human beings involved and upon a commitment to continuous education and development. The new way of working Toyota invented shifted the moods and predispositions of people and companies, the way that action was signaled and brought in, how bookkeeping and accounting was done, and how continuous improvement and continuous learning were produced in Toyota and its suppliers alike. A myriad of other features of their work were transformed.

The new style of working made possible a famous event. Following a fire in a supplier's plant that destroyed Toyota's entire supply of a critical part of their automotive brakes (and the capacity to build the part), Toyota was back in full production within a week. They were able to do this because their suppliers joined together to build the part — "P-valves" — for them in many shops and plants. (Toyota's competitors in the West, celebrating the event, had estimated that it would take Toyota the best part of a year to recover.)[4]

That is where the particular relevance of this little book begins to appear. In the 1980s, Hal Macomber began studying the manufacturing innovations that came out of the work of Ohno and Shingo, long before the term Lean was coined. Hal has been one of the most effective speakers in bringing the term Lean into common usage, particularly in the world of construction. And he became convinced that the experience of Ohno and Shingo could be deeply relevant to the challenge of improving the situation in Western industry. If you're anywhere

---

[4] Nishiguchi, T., & Beaudet, A. (1998). The Toyota Group and the Aisin Fire. *http://sloanreview.mit.edu/*. Retrieved from http://sloanreview.mit.edu/

near the construction industry and hear the term Lean from someone, the odds are very high that the source came in direct or indirect contact with Hal and Greg's work. One of the people who encountered Hal's experience and teaching was Calayde, who after many frustrations and failures in adopting Lean practices was looking for guidance herself. In embarking on the project of *The Pocket Sensei* together, they embody the heart of what they understand as Lean, engaging in collaborative learning experiences where the ultimate goal goes beyond improving project outcomes, processes, and products.

While the authors employ the word Lean in the book, *The Pocket Sensei* is really about the strong foundations that led to Toyota's innovations and not merely what we have come to call Lean in the States. The book offers 40 little exercises that give the serious practitioner an opportunity to sample and experience the deeply grounded principles and thinking that Ohno and Shingo employed in building their production system, along with its myriad techniques and innovations. This can be a good starting point for cultivating the new kinds of skills and sensibilities that Hal and I learned to pay attention to when we worked with our teacher Fernando Flores.[5]

The central weaknesses in our industries today are embodied in and generated by habitual ways of thinking, speaking, and acting found throughout the West. Those habits come largely from poor interpretations about (a) what human beings are and what we do, and (b) the way that we construct our lives and practices in language. As we observe people coordinating action in all parts of the world (including investing, financing, building, staffing, designing, commissioning, and so forth), we fail to recognize three critical things that underlie the efficacy of everything that happens.

First, the people — and not the contracts, methods, machines, procedures, processes, programs, rules, organizations, plans, or incentives — are responsible for producing action. What makes the difference is the creative and inventive capability of autonomous, responsible, competent human beings, working together to take care of concerns that they have inherited, appropriated, and invented.

Second, before anything else, everything happens out of people speaking and listening to each other. The great majority of mistakes, misdirections, and misunderstandings begin and are played out from miscoordinations generated in our speaking and listening to each other.

---

[5] https://en.wikipedia.org/wiki/Fernando_Flores

Finally, before we think or act, human beings are already pointed in directions by our moods and emotional predispositions. The effects of the worst of these predispositions — for example mistrust, resentment, skepticism, overwhelm, confusion, or frustration — are fair game for complaints and explaining failures, but are never included in the designs of how work is to be done. Yet they are far more powerful in determining outcomes than any other aspect of the work of coordination. Some predispositions (as named above) damage collaboration. Other predispositions, like passion, ambition, and humility, energize and focus participants. Consider the effect of trust on coordination in a team: without trust, it is often impossible to get anything worthwhile done. With trust, work proceeds more quickly, and vast simplifications are often possible. People and teams with the right training can and do adjust their predispositions to fit the challenges of their circumstances.

When my children were youngsters and studying Tai Kwando, their teacher showed us the way that simple moves — as in the *katas* described in the book — when repeated many times, led to the development of physical, mental, and emotional predispositions, skills, and sensibilities that were powerful in life. I saw that this was a wise characterization.

Now you have in front of you 40 *katas* designed for your working life. If you follow the instructions and take what you get from the experiences, you will be in far better shape to prepare yourself and others for the challenging work in whatever is your industry, which desperately needs new leadership.

How do you understand the moods you are in while your team faces their problems? How do you change your own mind? How do many people appear to be listening but are not, or are not being heard, are observing but have no idea what to do about what they are seeing? How many people don't even know how to look for, or offer improvements at all? How many opportunities might we have to improve ourselves, our relationships, and our companies, if we had what the book calls 'Lean leaders everywhere — on all organizational levels'?

Enjoy the experience of *The Pocket Sensei*. Join in the effort to change the way your organization engages with itself, your own work, and your relationships with others.

Good hunting!

— **Chauncey Bell**
Chairman and Chief of Design at Harvester & Co.

Welcome to

THE DOJO

What do you want to learn today?

HOW TO USE THIS BOOK.

We wrote this book to bring the wisdom of the fathers of Lean management and leadership to those of us who are practicing Lean leadership today. Much has been written in the last 15 years on Lean thinking. Long before the contemporary books were the key writings of two people who first-hand created the *Toyota Production System*. Those two people are Taiichi Ohno and Dr. Shigeo Shingo. They are the masters — the men that embodied the thinking, the philosophy, and the perspectives for what we now call Lean management. While we can no longer learn at the feet of the masters, we can put their wisdom into practice as routines that will be available to us when we need their wisdom the most.

Over the past 30 years Hal has read and re-read the masters' works, which have continued to be an inspiration and compass to him to this day. This first volume presents 40 selected quotations as representative of some of the masters' knowledge.

The book is structured in a simple way. There are five Parts, each with eight lessons and *katas*. Each quotation is followed by a short narrative lesson — an interpretation of the significance and relevance of the masters' knowledge to us in today's world. Each lesson is accompanied by one of Calayde's illustrations. The illustrations show fun, sometimes absurd, but optimistic situational stories — designed to set a cheerful mood and tie a series of eight *katas* together. The five stories, one for each Part of the book, tell a little tale of frustration, failure, or success. As the characters face and solve their problems to complete their stories, so too will you. Each time you practice your *katas* on this Lean journey, you will have different stories to tell.

People who study the martial arts, visual, or musical arts recognize that there is a rich, meaningful history embodied in the instructional language of these arts. In this volume, we use many Japanese words in homage to that tradition.

Let's start with the word *sensei* (sen-say). It means teacher. In eastern cultures, teacher is a revered position. To call someone *sensei*, is to show great respect for the person. We use *sensei* to show our respect for the Lean masters and to help you, the student, engage with these masters in a new way.

We also use the word *kata* (kah—tah). This means routine, practice, or exercise that, when performed, is intended to embody the masters' wisdom. Each *kata* is meant to be practiced and practiced again. It is through repetition that the wisdom and skill will become naturally available to you as an intuitive action. If you saw the movie *The Karate Kid,* you'll remember Miyagi, Daniel's *sensei,* had him perform the tasks (*kata*s) "wax the car," "paint the fence," and "sand the floor." Daniel begrudgingly performed those tasks, eventually getting frustrated that he wasn't getting any direct instruction from his teacher. However, when the teacher tested Daniel, the *kata*s produced the intended karate behaviors. Similarly, our *kata*s are designed to produce a shift in perspective and develop your intuitive and active skills.

Each instruction ends with *hansei* (hahn-say) — a reflection for the student to bring attention to what he or she is learning. It is with self-assessment and mindfulness that we intentionally develop new behaviors. Make a point of noting your reflections at the end of each *kata* and book Part. And, don't only reflect afterwards — also be mindful while you are in the action taking place. Take time out every so often to note the overall progress you are making and mark the routines you've completed in *The Dojo* in this book. Practice the *hansei*'s every time you perform the *kata*s.

Your *Toolkit* has many handy items for you to use, one of which is a brief glossary. When words are italicized, or unfamiliar to you, you can look these words up here in the glossary. The first time we introduce a new word, we will remind you with an * so you'll remember to go read about it. However, the deeper concepts are best described by the original authors, and you can find them in the reference sections of the *Toolkit.* We encourage you to pick up one or two of these items for your education as well — after all, they are the *senseis* to us all.

You will notice we ask you to observe your mood or the mood of others in many of the *hansei*'s. Why mood? How might observing mood be useful? The word is often used by making characterizations of oneself or others. "He's in a bad mood," or, "I'm in a cheerful mood." These characterizations at first appear merely descriptive of a person's emotional state. However, we are using the word in a richer way. We are asking after you perform a *kata* to make assessments of your outlook or disposition towards the future. Having finished trying something new, are you ambitious to do more? Or, are you humbled by how much there is to learn? Or, are you resolute to stay with the *kata* until it becomes second nature for you? Ambitious, humbled, and resolute are three possible moods you may encounter. You will surely find yourself in other moods too. Use these lessons to learn about your own and others' moods, and reflect on how the *katas* and moods interact as you move through situations.

You will discover that moods are neither good nor bad. They are, however, useful or not useful to you in accomplishing your objectives with Lean leadership and everything else in life! So, choose your moods wisely. They will help you stay focused on your goals. (See the *Toolkit: On Moods* to learn more.)

Each chapter finishes with a journal page for you to record your reflections, goal-setting, or for developing your lists of sayings and *kata*s. Use these pages to develop your own path to mastery. Draw and write all over this book. It is your journal — it belongs to you. Put your name on it.

We've arranged the lessons and *kata*s by stages in your development as a Lean leader. In Part I, *Be a beginner,* you will learn simple but fundamental practices. As you move through the lessons, you will learn about your important work as you *Get selfish* in Part II, and how to *Bring others along with you* in Part III. You and your partners will *Bring focus to all your efforts* in Part IV, and finally, learn how to *Embrace contradictions* with Part V. Each Part starts and finishes with a call to challenge you and lead you to practicing mindful actions within your projects and work.

Don't restrict yourself with our organization of the lessons. Experiment by taking different paths through the book. Do you immediately want to signal that "things are now different around here"? Start with *Gary's Office Kata* to increase your frequency of visiting the place of the real work. Move on to the *30-Minute Gemba Kata* to generate a flurry of waste reductions. Finish with the *Improvement Kata* to focus a small group in rapidly achieving a step-change in their performance. In just three weeks, you will have noticeably altered your routines to the extent that others will not only notice that, their routines will be altered, too.

Record your progress at the beginning of the book in *The Dojo*, by ticking off the first five times you perform a *kata* and *hansei*. See how you progress, make your way through this content as much as you can. This is your path to mastery.

We are very interested in hearing about you using *The Pocket Sensei* to develop your Lean leadership. Please share your successes and your challenges with us. It will help us and other readers learn more from the Lean masters.

Ohno and Shingo left us with a rich legacy that continues to guide us in becoming informed as we set out to remake our companies to be fleet-footed and value-focused individuals and organizations. Treat yourself to a reading of one of their books too. There is a reference list at the end of this book of the texts we used and a few other texts that may interest you too.

Finally, please visit *www.thepocketsensei.com* for more resources and *kata*s.

We've done our best to create *kata*s that, when practiced routinely, will produce a shift in how you engage in the world. We can say that many of them worked for us — and we hope they work for you too.

Enjoy this journey!

— Hal Macomber & Calayde Davey

THE DOJO

What do you want to learn today?

Special Acknowledgment   x
Forword   xiii
How to use this book.   xxi

THE DOJO
Introduction   3

PART I
Be a beginner.   5

PART II
Get selfish — an hour a day for your important work.   41

PART III
Bring others along with you.   77

PART IV
Bring focus to all your efforts.   113

PART V
Embrace contradictions.   149

Afterword   185
Special Thanks   187

TOOLKIT
On Moods   190
A3 Thinking and Learning   193
Advanced Ohno Circle - 30 Minutes | 30 Wastes | 30 Days   194
Five Whys - Traditional   195
Good 5-Why - Branching Process   196
Glossary   198
References   199

PART I
Be a beginner.

Part I
Be a beginner.   5

Practice Board

○ ○ ○ ○ ○   **1. Give new ideas a chance.**   **9**
     Counter-FUD Kata   10

○ ○ ○ ○ ○   **2. Confirm failure with your own eyes.**   **13**
     Variance Kata   24

○ ○ ○ ○ ○   **3. Take action immediately**
     if a defect is detected.   **17**
     Swarm Kata   18

○ ○ ○ ○ ○   **4. Make only what you can sell.**   **21**
     Pie Kata   22

○ ○ ○ ○ ○   **5. Don't be afraid of lost opportunities.**   **25**
     Candy Store Kata   26

○ ○ ○ ○ ○   **6. Dissatisfaction is the**
     'mother' of improvement.   **29**
     My Dissatisfaction Kata   30

○ ○ ○ ○ ○   **7. People who are satisfied with**
     the way things are can never achieve
     improvement or progress.   **33**
     Our Dissatisfaction Kata   34

○ ○ ○ ○ ○   **8. Never accept the status quo.**   **37**
     No Status Quo Kata   38

PART II

Get selfish — an hour a day for your important work.

Part II

Get selfish — an hour a day
for your important work.   41

Practice Board

9. Transportation is a crime.   **45**
     Magic Roundabout Kata   46

**10. The source of information is
always the customer.**   **49**
     Their Dissatisfaction Kata   50

11. Wasted motion is not work.   **53**
     Value / Motion Kata   54

12. Small minds want more space.   **57**
     Promise Kata   58

**13. If you don't know why defects
are occurring, make some defects.**   **61**
     Good 5-Why Kata   62

**14. We must always grasp the real facts —
i.e., what is — rather than what ought to be.**   **65**
     Gary's Office Kata   66

**15. We must dig up the real cause by asking
why, why, why, why, why.**   **69**
     5 Why = 1 How Kata   70

16. The same as yesterday isn't good enough.   **73**
     New World Kata   74

PART III

Bring others along with you.

Part III

Bring others along with you. 77

Practice Board

○○○○○ **17. Our invariable response to, "It can't be done" is, "Do it!"** **81**
Extreme Why Kata 82

○○○○○ **18. Illusions can easily turn into conventional wisdom.** **85**
Scientific Kata 86

○○○○○ **19. Distinguish between movement and work to cultivate the ability to find waste.** **89**
Motion / Work Kata 90

○○○○○ **20. The greatest waste is the waste we don't see.** **93**
8th Waste Kata 94

○○○○○ **21. Before anything else, give it a try.** **97**
PDSA Kata 98

○○○○○ **22. We must exhaustively pursue our true objectives — the abstract objects lying beyond what is visible.** **101**
What Matters Kata 102

○○○○○ **23. Rationalize your operation when business is booming.** **105**
Good Times Kata 106

○○○○○ **24. The medicine won't work unless you take it.** **109**
Multivitamin Kata 110

PART IV

Bring focus to all your efforts.

Part IV

Bring focus to all your efforts.   113

Practice Board

( ) ( ) ( ) ( ) ( )   **25. We will not be able to blaze new trails
unless we boldly turn our thinking processes
upside down, and unless everyone participates
in that revolution.**   **117**

Mars Kata   118

( ) ( ) ( ) ( ) ( )   **26. We use checklists so not to forget
that we have forgotten.**   **121**

Parachute Kata   122

( ) ( ) ( ) ( ) ( )   **27. Find problems where you think
none exist.**   **125**

Variable Kata   126

( ) ( ) ( ) ( ) ( )   **28. Everyone confuses motion with work.**   **129**

Stop / Motion Kata   130

( ) ( ) ( ) ( ) ( )   **29. Usually mass production raises costs.**   **133**

Change-over Kata   134

( ) ( ) ( ) ( ) ( )   **30. The best way to clean something is to
make sure it doesn't get dirty in the
first place.**   **137**

Ship-shape Kata   138

( ) ( ) ( ) ( ) ( )   **31. Stand on the production floor all day
and watch — eventually you will discover
what has to be done.**   **141**

30 Min Gemba Kata   142

( ) ( ) ( ) ( ) ( )   **32. All our knowledge and understanding
won't get us anywhere unless we are able
to act on it.**   **145**

Laboratory Kata   146

PART V

Embrace contradictions.

Part V

Embrace contradictions. 149

Practice Board

○ ○ ○ ○ ○ **33. If we don't understand what it is that we don't understand, we have no idea what to do about it.** 153

Mind-field Kata 154

○ ○ ○ ○ ○ **34. "Know-how" alone isn't enough! You need to "know-why!"** 157

Know-Why Kata 158

○ ○ ○ ○ ○ **35. Understanding alone isn't enough to get people moving.** 161

My Hypothesis Kata 162

○ ○ ○ ○ ○ **36. We act on what we think is true. Don't act on assumptions.** 165

Our Hypothesis Kata 166

○ ○ ○ ○ ○ **37. Find waste!** 169

Two Great Wastes Kata 170

○ ○ ○ ○ ○ **38. "Eliminate waste!" is a nonsensical slogan.** 173

Waste Finder Kata 174

○ ○ ○ ○ ○ **39. When carrying out improvements, you will only be truly effective when you first set your objectives and then head straight for them.** 177

Improvement Kata 178

○ ○ ○ ○ ○ **40. Never say, "Impossible."** 181

Mission Possible Kata 182

The Pocket SENSEI

Mastering Lean Leadership
with 40 Katas

• VOLUME I •

Hal Macomber & Calayde Davey

thepocketsensei.com

INTRODUCTION

So you've found yourself thrust into a new role — a very challenging role — a role where many people fail. We intend to turn the odds of success in your favor. The role of a Lean leader is pivotal to the success of your company's Lean journey and ultimately the success of the company as a whole. Lean leaders are needed at all organizational levels and throughout all projects.

You can learn about Lean practices from many sources: books, articles, seminars, conferences and many more. We encourage you to do many or all of those things. In our canvassing of available resources, we couldn't find any help for the most challenging aspect of your role: being a Lean leader example while being an open learner. Frankly, you can't be a Lean leader without being an open learner. There is no place to go to learn that. Your job awaits.

Hal has been working with Lean leaders going back to the mid 1980's. He's been reading, studying, and experimenting with clients and colleagues for all that time. With this book we are returning to the wisdom of the Lean founders as an introduction to a set of routines or practices. We call them *kata*s — they will get you started on a path to mastering your new role.

We are not the *sensei's*. Taiichi Ohno and Shigeo Shingo are your *sensei's*. While we set out to offer our interpretation of their wisdom, we urge you to make your own sense from their knowledge too.

Most people who take on a role of Lean leadership do so while fulfilling some other full-time role in the company or project. Success will depend in part on creating supportive environments for learning and mastery. All learning requires practice in a setting that is tolerant to failure. You can create that setting by engaging your network of friends and colleagues to support your learning.

Journaling is an important practice for getting on a path to mastery. It allows you to increase what you notice is happening to you and in your environment. It also provides a basis for assessing how observation skills are changing through time. Finally, it serves as a record of your thoughts that will be invaluable for reflection. In this book, we provided pages for journaling, however you may elect to get a small notebook that you can carry with you expressly for the purpose of working on the exercises.

Develop your own path of mastery. Start with a reflection on your current operations or business. What is going on today that dominates your attention? What is challenging the company that needs more attention? However you work through the book and practice the *kata*s, have fun with it. Enjoy your successes. Marvel at your surprises. Be gentle on yourself with your difficulties. And be generous with your interpretations when encountering resistance from others.

It's a journey for us all.

JOURNAL

PART I

Be a beginner.

When we are learning, we are making mistakes. That is just the way it is. It's called being a beginner. Go easy on yourself. Make learning enjoyable. See the humor when things are more difficult than you had anticipated. The more you practice a *kata*, the fewer mistakes you'll make — until you start working on another *kata*! Look forward to that time when you set yourself back on a steep learning curve. It will make you the Lean leader you want to be. Enjoy the result of your hard work.

Throughout the book we encourage you to create a supportive environment for your learning. Keeping a journal is one of those actions. Getting a learning buddy is another. Pick someone who is generally supportive of what you do. It could be someone at work or outside of work too. If the person can join with you, all the better. At a minimum get someone you can speak with comfortably about what you are learning and what you find challenging.

Another thing you can do is tell people what you are doing. Don't keep it a secret. Your Lean initiative certainly isn't a secret. Make your personal goals public and invite people to help you. You might be surprised how many people support you with their actions.

Let's get going!

JOURNAL

JOURNAL

Give new ideas a chance.

1

Give new ideas a chance.

Taiichi Ohno

When a new idea is presented we often hear people say, "That won't work." But there is something worse than having colleagues, friends or family take shots at your ideas. Worse is when we tell ourselves that our idea is no good.

So your idea is not ready to be implemented. So what? Give new ideas a chance. As Lean leaders, we will never create the conditions ripe for innovation and learning in our organization if we don't first learn to challenge our own fear, uncertainty, and doubt — or as marketing and software professionals like to call it: FUD. The expression "we are our own worst enemy" rings true. Fear, uncertainty, and doubt (FUD) is a habit — a bad habit.

Fear, uncertainty and doubt keeps us from pursuing our dreams and ambitions, and worse, it gets in the way of what we care about most. We want the people in our lives to do well, be well and be supported in their dreams. Every day there are the germs of ideas that can grow into the big ideas that will take care of our own concerns and our concerns for others — if we just give ideas a chance.

Fear and doubt — particularly self-doubt — are quite familiar to most. But what about uncertainty? Uncertainty arises from what we don't know about our current situation and what we can't know about the future. Uncertainty is the basis of financial speculation, all games of chance, and the wonder of life. Uncertainty won't go away, but you can have a different approach to dealing with the unknown — and unknowable.

What is the opposite of FUD? Bravery, wonder and confidence. Let's explore how to break the FUD habit. Let's create a new relationship with our new ideas and the new ideas of others.

Counter-FUD Kata

Giving new ideas a chance starts with noticing new ideas, specifically those ideas that you may typically immediately discount. When a new idea comes up — good, bad, or indifferent — simply write it down. For any new idea, catch yourself when you worry about imagined negative consequences. Catch yourself when you don't see how anything could work. Catch yourself in your doubting moments. Make a note of each hesitation or question.

Now, turn each note around. What positive consequences can you see? How much better off could you or others be with this new idea? What might help you make a change? What do you need to learn? Whose help could you use? What could bring you confidence?

In this new state of bravery, wonder and confidence, who will you speak with about this idea?

Repeat the exercise throughout the week.

Hansei

Write a note to yourself about replacing the fear, uncertainty and doubt (FUD) habit with the bravery, wonder, and confidence (BWC) habit. What will your life be like when you have the habit of giving new ideas a chance? How do you see the BWC habit shifting your relationships? How will your job be different?

JOURNAL

Confirm failure with your own eyes.

2

Confirm failure with your own eyes.

Taiichi Ohno

Failure is a wonderful gift. In reply to a *New York Times* reporter's question on failure, Thomas Edison said: "I have not failed 700 times. I have succeeded in proving that those 700 ways will not work. When I have eliminated the ways that will not work, I will find the way that will work."[1] Accelerating our learning requires that we see failure with our own eyes.

Ohno called this practice *genchi genbutsu*,* seeing for yourself at the place of the real work — or *gemba**. It is at the work setting where we can get first-hand facts. Going to *gemba* helps us separate facts from interpretations, speculations, and preconceived notions.

Seeing with our own eyes is not as good as seeing with others' eyes. Your own perspective is highly limited and subjective. *Genchi genbutsu* is better performed with others, particularly when looking at failures or errors. We can bring people with different experiences and perspectives together and investigate what one person alone is not likely to understand.

Failure is not the only time we want to confirm a situation with our own eyes. Failure may happen only once in awhile. However, variances occur frequently. We use the word variance to mean "something different from our expectation." Each variance, anomaly, difficulty, and problem is an opportunity to learn something that would otherwise not be learned. But, you will not learn if you don't go to see for yourself.

Our challenge as Lean leaders is to get people everywhere to announce their variances, problems, and failures. We live in a world where people have learned to just deal with the problems they encounter by "making do"[2] never raising the issue for others to see. We also live in a world where people are embarrassed (or fear punishment) when they make mistakes. Making do and keeping quiet are coping mechanisms that block learning from variances, let alone failure.

See Toolkit: Glossary

Variance Kata

There are two parts to this routine. First, make a point of sharing one of your variances with someone you work with. Do it in the mood of "This is interesting — what can we learn together?" Explore what was at the root of the variance. Keep your attention on learning, not blaming. Commit to take action if you discover a root cause. Finish by thanking the person for investigating the variance with you.

The second part is to invite that person to share a variance with you in the future. Commit to be ready to investigate the variance or problem at the place and as close to the time the variance occurred.

Hansei

How was the exercise for you? What did you learn? What mood were you in when you shared your variance or problem? What mood was the other person in? How did your mood change during the *kata*? How confident are you that the other person will share a variance with you? Why?

JOURNAL

Take action immediately if a defect is detected.

3

Take action immediately if a defect is detected.

Shigeo Shingo

Dr. Shingo instructs us to act immediately when discovering a defect. Let's first understand why, and then what kind of action to take. Shingo wrote the book *Zero Quality Control*.[3] One device Shingo used for error-proofing production was to establish a discipline of successively checking through the process for defects. In Shingo's world, defects are gems.

A defect presents the opportunity to learn about how the process is failing. Learning is best done with the people who were witness to the defect, at the place where it occurred, and as close to the moment that the defect occurred. This brings together four of the Toyota Way principles: build a culture of stopping to fix problems; respect for people; continuous process improvement; and go and see for yourself.

Everyone in operations needs to know that it is their responsibility to announce defects, variances, anomalies, and problems at the moment they detect them. You are not simply giving them the opportunity to raise these issues. You are not simply open to listen to the problems your colleagues find. Lean leaders insist that everyone must call attention to defects. Anything less than that is unacceptable behavior. Being individually resourceful — working around problems, keeping defects and errors to oneself, or making do — is one thing. Getting others to announce defects and problems is another. We don't imply that it will be easy to shift behavior from individual resourcefulness to group resourcefulness. It may be your greatest challenge.

What do the masters want us to do? Shingo and others want us to "swarm the problem."[4] Swarming is about learning immediately from what just happened or what was just discovered. It recognizes the perishability of the data and knowledge of the incident. It also represents the senior commitment to driving all waste from the system when people stop whatever they are doing to do the important work of the company.

Swarm Kata

This *kata* will focus on getting people to announce their problems. In *Kata #15* you will learn more about getting to root causes.

Start with supervisory staff. Ask to be immediately informed when a defect occurs. Make a promise that you will come immediately to see the defect for yourself. Immediately stop what you are doing when you get the call. Go to the work area. Thank people for calling you. Begin asking about the defect. Do a simple 5-whys if you are able. Spend just enough time to learn, but not so much time that you further disrupt the operations. Thank people again when you leave.

Be always well-prepared for the moment a defect comes about so you are not delayed getting to the place of the defect. For example, have your personal protective equipment always ready. Either clear your schedule for the week, or let people know that you will be taking calls during meetings and that you will leave to investigate defects.

Hansei

What hurdles did you encounter to act immediately when defects occurred? How did you overcome them? What did you learn about the work and the people? How did they respond to your new behavior? What improvements, if any, resulted from your actions?

JOURNAL

Make only what you can sell.

4

Make only what you can sell.

Taiichi Ohno

Making only what we sell or consume is contrary to our modern common sense. Isn't it true that making two pies is almost as easy as making one pie? Certainly the bake time is no longer. Preparation and clean-up are about the same. So, three pies would be better — right? What about ten pies? How many pies can we make at once? And, how many pies can we eat at once? How many pies will get spoiled because we can't eat them quickly enough? Suddenly, baking ten pies is making us think differently about how easy it is to make many pies at once — and how hard it is to make sure all the pies get eaten and no pie is wasted.

Why is it easy to make more than what we can consume or sell? It has to do with the setting up and breaking down processes. Getting the kitchen ready for baking, grabbing and sorting utensils, or assembling the ingredients, are all "make-ready" tasks. These are tasks that take about the same time to perform for one pie as they do for two or ten pies. But what if the time to perform those tasks was so insignificant that we could bake a pie at any time we wanted? Wouldn't that change how we thought about making just what we could consume?

Making more than we consume or sell just to avoid setting up and cleaning up (mobilizing and demobilizing) comes with other costs and wastes. We need a larger investment in pie plates. We need a larger area to cool the pies. We need someplace to store the finished pies so they won't spoil before we consume them. And if we are making ahead for many foods like cakes, brownies and custards, we will need a tracking system so we know what to eat and by when. None of these investments produces more value for us. In fact, if we misjudge what we will consume then we can have waste of the finished item.

Taiichi Ohno advises us to make just what we sell. Improving the make-ready work helps us avoid wasted inventory, along with all the hidden costs and efforts supporting that inventory. Making just what we sell requires us to frequently set up and break down every time we want to consume. The better you get at that, the more opportunities you create for improvements and eliminating waste.

Pie Kata

Start with one item that you currently make in batches larger than the sales quantity for that day or week. Now, cut that batch in half or to the actual sales quantity, whichever is greater. What systems or processes break along the way? Get to work on improvements so you can continue to "make only what you can sell."

As you approach unit-of-one production, what investments are no longer needed? What tooling and equipment become excess? How much can inventory be reduced? How much less storage do you need?

Repeat this for another item, and another, and another.

Hansei

Where do you see this approach will take your firm? How much capital will it free up? What will that do for your costs? How will it distinguish you from your competitors? What is needed to adopt "make only what you can sell" more widely?

JOURNAL

Don't be afraid of lost opportunities.

5

Don't be afraid of lost opportunities.

Taiichi Ohno

One of my childhood friends could go to a candy store and come out without having spent his money. The rest of us were sucking on root beer barrels, chewing on Squirrel Nuts,† and blowing bubbles with wads of bubble gum. Not him. He struggled spending his money on one item when it would keep him from spending it on another item. No root beer barrels for him if it meant he wouldn't have money left for Squirrel Nuts. This is known as the loss aversion bias. It is one of many biases that leads to the ineffective allocation of time and money.

That we can't have a Squirrel Nut if we spend our money elsewhere negates any rewards we could receive by spending a resource elsewhere. Committing our time, effort, and resources on one endeavor to the exclusion of other endeavors ensures that what matters will get done. It is challenging as individuals. Even more so in organizations.

We must focus our efforts on those things that matter most. Deciding that I should work on improving one thing keeps me from improving another thing. Should I do it? Working on two or more improvements at once — task switching — only delays the completion of both. How is any person to make the choice of what to do at any point in time?

Toyota does this for everyone in the company through a process called *hoshin kanri.** It is a process of top-down and bottom-up strategic planning. The planning results in two or three essential goals that, when met, will set Toyota apart from their competitors.

A few years ago in North America, Toyota's *hoshin kanri** process produced two goals: (1) to have a net positive impact on the environment everywhere Toyota does business and (2) to reduce repairs made under warranty by 80%. These two goals focused all staff improvement efforts. While not excluding work in other areas (staff still had the opportunity to make their work safer, easier or more interesting) *hoshin* goals make it very clear what is important to the company as a whole, and what are for now just Squirrel Nuts.

**See Toolkit: Glossary*

†*A Squirrel Nut Chew is made of caramel and peanuts. They were 1¢ when Hal was a child.*

Candy Store Kata

Start each day by committing to one goal that is important to you and the company, but not urgent. Carve out one full hour in your schedule to work on that goal. Don't be distracted by other matters. They will still be there at the end of the hour. Do this for two full weeks.

Invite one or two others to take up this practice joining you in pursuing the same goal. Do this for another two weeks.

Hansei

Along the way, reflect on the progress you are making. Are you feeling a sense of accomplishment? Are you keeping up with other matters? Where are you after two weeks? Four weeks? What do you predict the few of you will have accomplished in a month? A quarter?

What will you have to stop doing to continue to make the time to focus on this goal? As you progress with this *kata*, how will you expand this practice to focus the organization on the essential company goals?

JOURNAL

Dissatisfaction is the 'mother' of improvement.

6

Dissatisfaction is the 'mother' of improvement.

Shigeo Shingo

Fast Company did a feature article in December 2006 titled "No Satisfaction at Toyota."[5] This was one of the first articles on Toyota that wasn't written from an engineering or manufacturing perspective. The focus was on the mood of Toyota employees. That mood was described as "always a little dissatisfied." Contrast this mood with the mood found in all too many companies — the "good-enough" mood.

Our mood of dissatisfaction shows up not by whining and complaining, rather it is in our everyday actions. It is in the paper clip that we pick off the floor, the picture that we straighten on the wall, and the exposed screw that we cover so no one is hurt. The mood of dissatisfaction is the constant mindset of "this can be better today than it was yesterday." That mindset is not just important, it separates your business from all others. The author wrote:

> *"Continuous improvement is tectonic. By constantly questioning how you do things, by constantly tweaking, you don't outflank your competition next quarter. You outflank them next decade."*

Dr. Shingo calls dissatisfaction the "mother" of improvement. What he doesn't say is you can cultivate dissatisfaction in your staff. It takes a little prodding, encouragement, demonstration of one's own dissatisfaction, and determination in the face of slow progress.

My Dissatisfaction Kata

You start, as usual, by working on yourself. Cultivate your dissatisfaction through your daily actions. It starts with noticing that things are just a little out of place and you can and will do something about it. What is out of place? Use that question as you go about your day's work. Look for opportunities to make small adjustments and then make those adjustments. Do this day after day for at least a week.

Next, focus on noticing and writing down specific things about how your work could be a little better, a little safer, a little easier, or a little more interesting to perform. This is called *Quick 'n Easy Kaizen.** What small problem do you notice? What small change can you make to eliminate that problem? How is your work safer, easier or more interesting as a result? Remember, focus on your work, not the work of others. Make at least one small improvement every day for at least a week. Record that improvement answering the questions: what problem do I have? What change did I make? How did it get better?

Hansei

Make notes here on what you notice as you go about adjusting the world and making small improvements to your work. What do you notice about your mood? What reaction are you noticing in others?

---

*See Toolkit: Glossary

JOURNAL

*People who are satisfied with the way things are
can never achieve improvement or progress.*

7

People who are satisfied with the way things are can never achieve improvement or progress.

Shigeo Shingo

It is said that "best is the enemy of better." However, complacency breeds mediocrity, leading to degrading performance.

There is a not-so-fine line between "good enough for now" and complacency. That line is about the definition of *now*. Is *now* once through the process? Or is *now* until the end of the month? End of the Quarter? End of the project? "Good enough for now" coupled with *Plan-Do-Study-Act (PDSA)*[10]* will lead to spiraling improvements.

On a visit Hal made to NUMMI, he heard from a Human Resources person that Toyota hires people who are just a little dissatisfied with the status quo. They look for people who pick up a paper clip, who straighten a picture or who wipe down a wet counter-top. These are people who are not complainers looking for someone else to take action. No — these people are dissatisfied enough to take action without direction.

In 1989, Dr. John (as he was known by his employees), wrote a little book for them to share his personal philosophy behind the success of J.P. Industries. This little book, *Better Makes Us Best,*[6] brought a focus and imperative to make today just a little better than yesterday.

Dr. John's approach was simple: be clear about the destination; set interim goals; track progress; and do a little better today than you did yesterday. What isn't simple is bringing this to life in your organization. That requires engaged, patient and determined leadership. Dr. John provided that leadership. You can too.

Toyota uses *hoshin kanri* to develop big goals that are universally communicated, ensures that progress is tracked, and that every supervisor supports their team in their daily work by asking, "How will we do better today than yesterday?"

---

*See Toolkit: Glossary

Our Dissatisfaction Kata

First, identify a big objective for your project, your business unit, or your small group. Next, share that big goal with your staff or colleagues to identify a first interim goal that is challenging yet attainable. Put all this to paper. Now, start each day in a conversation with your team reviewing what they did yesterday to advance the goal and what they will do today to be better than yesterday. Celebrate the small wins. As Dr. John said, "There are no small ideas." The freedom and dissatisfaction with the current situation to offer up small, ill-formed or half-baked ideas will lead to big wins over the long term. Nurture that environment with the question, "How will we do better today than yesterday?"

Hansei

How is your small group or team responding to your new engagement with their work, their future, and their contributions? What has been easy for you? What has been difficult? Why do you suppose it is difficult? Who might help you with this?

Make notes daily of your progress. How has your mood supported you in this effort? What might you do to continue with a supportive mood or shift to a more supportive mood? What will you do?

JOURNAL

Never accept the status quo.

8

Never accept the status quo.

Shigeo Shingo

Not so long ago, Hal had a house built in the White Mountains of New Hampshire. It's the only house he had built. It was to be their retirement house. While they have access to just about anything anyone could want, the standard practices of the local construction industry weren't keeping up with other areas of the country. Further, being in the construction industry himself, he brought higher expectations to his own project than the local status quo.

Hal didn't set out to do something exotic. He just wanted to use standard energy efficient construction details in use throughout the country. His problems started with the foundation. The builder wanted to do a traditional poured concrete foundation. However, only a few miles up the road, a friend of Hal's built a house with a pre-cast foundation. That foundation went in quickly, had a very high insulating value, and was cost neutral. It would have been easier to accept the status quo of Hal's builder, but Hal didn't. Instead, he insisted on the better product and installed a pre-cast foundation.

Construction problems continued. One detail after another wasn't constructed according to plan, although the problems were always "workable." Hal didn't accept it. It was tough being pleasant while being dissatisfied.

Hal wanted to install a radiant in-ceiling heating system in the second floor bedrooms. The heating contractor didn't want to install the in-ceiling radiant heat. The builder told Hal he was making a mistake. Both the builder and the heating contractor didn't believe it would work. They were sure his guests would be cold during their -10° winters. They insisted that Hal sign a waiver of responsibility claiming that everyone knows that heat rises. (It doesn't. Hot air rises; heat radiates.) Hal didn't accept their status quo — he built the heated ceilings, and his guests love the comfortable bedrooms.

Dr. Shingo's admonition to never accept the status quo is not easy. Rejecting the status quo is not about luck or stubbornness. This mindset comes about by doing your homework and living in a state of dissatisfaction. Doing so requires attention to your mood and the moods of the people around you. Bad moods are contagious. Lean leaders can't be walking around in a bad mood. Still, being in a good mood while being dissatisfied is a challenge — one worth cultivating.

No Status Quo Kata

There are a number of exercises in this book about being a little dissatisfied. The *No Status Quo Kata* is a routine focusing on and maintaining your mood. If you are to believe Engineer Ohno and Dr. Shingo about complacency, dissatisfaction, and the status quo, then you have to attend to your mood. Do the following:

For a particular situation where you are dissatisfied with the status quo, choose a mood for yourself that will support advancing or improving the situation. (Refer to *On Moods* in the *Toolkit*). It might be a mood of ambition, one of experimentation or one of seriousness. Put yourself in that mood as you explore with others what you will do about your dissatisfaction. Notice any changes in your mood through the conversations.

Hansei

Could you adopt your chosen mood? If not, what was getting in your way? If so, how did it impact your result? How did others react to you? Record your thoughts.

JOURNAL

PART II

Get selfish —an hour a day for your important work.

It's easy to get caught up in the urgencies of the moment. Putting out fires can be gratifying work because it usually means solving a crisis. The problem is that there is always another fire to put out. While gratifying, we find this work emotionally draining. After a day of moving from one crisis to the next, Hal struggles to do the creative work that his consulting business requires. Further, it's easy to forget about his bigger goals and aspirations. This is not the way to produce mastery.

All top performers in any field know that you have to put the important work first. The important work is directly associated with your goals. Hal set a goal to get his first book published. He can't take two months out of his life to do the research, writing, editing, production, and promotion — Hal needs to stay engaged in his business too. What he can do is carve out one hour each day to work on his goal. Hal does that work in the first hour of the day. Early morning is a great time for him to write. His clients aren't awake, neither are his family or his colleagues. Hal knows he won't be interrupted.

Hal discovered this a few years ago. He started writing a blog on project management in 2001. While he was serious about it, his writing was hit or miss. Posting was erratic. Hal struggled to find topics to write about. Along the way he noticed that athletes and musicians don't leave their training to hit or miss. Athletes do their crunches and their push-ups whether they are competing or not. Taking care of their core is important work. Musicians practice studies every day to keep their agility. Hal put himself on a schedule. Eight years later he had published a thousand articles or posts.

For Hal, blogging has taken a backseat to writing this book. Blogging isn't his important work now. It may be again. You will see the same thing as you pursue mastery of Lean leadership. The *katas* will be important while you read them now, but you may lose your agility if you don't consider them as a part of your important work.

Many of the *katas* can be done as you go about your day. But don't rely on finding the time — you won't just find the time. In fact, your Lean journey is likely to create more demands on you. Developing oneself as a Lean leader is important work. Block out the time to practice this important work. It takes time. It takes attention. It deserves at least an hour a day. That hour doesn't need to be the same hour, but you need to schedule the hour. Make the time to succeed — just one hour.

JOURNAL

JOURNAL

Transportation is a crime

9

Transportation is a crime.

Shigeo Shingo

Engineer Ohno identified *7 Wastes**, one of which is *unnecessary transportation*. Dr. Shingo took it one step further — referring to transportation within production facilities as a crime. His point applies broadly — from production on a construction job site, to the hospital nursing floor, software design, and all sorts of administrative processing operations.

A rapidly growing part of the world economy is associated with machines for moving and handling materials within production facilities.[7] Beyond the machines, we have to add control systems, maintenance programs, fuel use, and labor to operate the equipment. None of that adds any value for the customer. None. You can see why Dr. Shingo calls transportation a crime.

The need for transportation arises from the thoughtless design of production lines, of the delivery and packaging of materials, and of the presentation of materials to the workers. The same is true of construction work sites. Too often production lines aren't designed for continuous *flow**. Materials are packaged and shipped without regard to how, where, and when the materials will be used. On too many construction sites an open space is an invitation for storage. Uncrating and stocking are required to make the material available at the point of use. None of that adds value for the customer.

If you visit a Toyota manufacturing facility, you will have to look hard to find forklifts. You'll have to look to see pallets of material too. Instead, you'll find incoming materials packaged in reusable totes that go directly to the point of use on the production line. The totes can be lifted by a single person generally without the aid of a machine. When empty, the tote becomes a request — *kanban* — to replenish production. It has taken Toyota decades to design transportation out of their operations. In any of your own operations, there is a very high chance of you committing a crime of transportation. How can you reduce these crimes?

See Toolkit: Glossary

Magic Roundabout Kata

Why are you using transportation today? Make an inventory of all the transport equipment, the people required to run that equipment, the energy costs to run the equipment, the maintenance costs, and the depreciation. Share that crime with the organization.

Next, begin an improvement process to eliminate transportation needs. It could take a rethinking of the supply chain. At a minimum you'll want to look at how material gets from the receiving area to the point of use (without packaging materials). You won't get rid of all transportation overnight, but a little better every day will lead to lower costs and speedier operations. Track the gains you make in a public way and revisit this *kata* weekly.

Hansei

What was your reaction to the total costs you incur for the crime of transportation? Others' reaction? What would be the impact on the business and for your customers of reducing transportation costs by 80%? What is keeping you from pursuing that goal? How will you enroll others?

JOURNAL

The source of information is always the customer.

10

The source of information is always the customer.

Taiichi Ohno

In 1985, while preparing for his first study mission to Japan, Hal was told that the word for "marketing" in Japan was a translation of the term *market-in*. Whether that was/is true or not, Ohno has a similar interesting perspective on the information available at the point of sale. Ohno's view is that the most knowledge available at any time, is that of the *"Now!"* Ohno says, "Whoever can best grasp and utilize *"Now!"* information will win."[8]

Ohno describes that, in the '70s and '80s, 7-Eleven Japan took a new approach. Contrary to their contemporaries, instead of studying what was selling, 7-Eleven decided to see what *doesn't* sell — and then make room for more of what is wanted by their customers. The general way to put this is, "What is it that we are doing or providing that is not satisfying to our customers?"

There are three ways of thinking about *customer*. The first is to think of the party that is buying our product or service. There are aspects of our product that provide value, other aspects that are not providing value, and still others that dissatisfy the *customer*. Amazon's Certified Frustration-Free Packaging is a result of responding to what wasn't valued and was dissatisfying.

A second view of *customer* is to think of the next group in the value stream. Our product might be part of a product that another entity is selling to their *customer*. The same three conditions apply: we provide value, no value, or we dissatisfy the *customer*. For example, consulting engineers provide services to architects that are bundled into a set of plans for an owner.

The third view of *customer* is to think of the next person in the process. In the course of doing our work, is the person doing the next step getting value, no value, or are they dissatisfied with our work product?

Anytime you are providing something that a *customer* doesn't value, you will find waste. Don't miss that opportunity to listen to your *customers'* dissatisfactions, to discover, and eliminate waste. Doing so creates capacity for providing greater value and building your reputation as an innovator — both as an individual and as a firm.

Their Dissatisfaction Kata

Don't wait for complaints, seek *customers'* dissatisfactions. Start your practice by organizing a conversation with someone performing the next step in a process. Explore what they value, don't value and what dissatisfies. Many people won't be comfortable in the conversation. They don't want to appear negative. You'll put them at ease in this conversation by being open, curious, and appreciative of their responses. Be sure to use follow-up questions to avoid misunderstanding. Always finish with a sincere thank you and a promise to report on the actions you will take.

Do this a few times before going to a customer who bundles your work into their work to learn about their dissatisfactions. Do this a few times before going to your end customer.

Hansei

What did you find in this dissatisfactions treasure hunt? Could you stay positive? Did you notice any of your own or others' defensiveness? Could you keep a positive mood for you and your customer? Make a note on what you will work on in your next conversation.

JOURNAL

Wasted motion is not work.

11

Wasted motion is not work.

Taiichi Ohno

When we move something that shouldn't have been present, we exert effort but we do not create any value. Taiichi Ohno reminds us that the purpose of "work" is to create or add value. When value is not created, he says, our motions (efforts) are not work.

Ohno is contradicting our commonsense understanding of work. In physics, for example, we say work has occurred when a force is applied to an object, and that object moves. Work increases by both 1) applying the force and 2) the object traveling a certain distance. However, Ohno is saying when we cause waste through motion, we don't necessarily cause work. To understand waste we need consider the result from the customer's perspective. Would the customer say that he has received more value as a result of the effort applied and the movement that occurred? If not, then that motion was wasted.

Consider the following: when we reach for something, we are not producing value, yet not reaching keeps us from producing value. When we must reposition ourselves to perform a task, the repositioning is waste. When we search for materials, the *customer* receives no more value than had it been readily available. From the physics perspective work may have occurred, but from the customer's perspective, the customer is no better off. And from the company's perspective, energy and time was expended, but the company gets no more revenue.

How about the work of engineers, programmers, artists, writers, managers, and others who don't do physical work? They certainly have the same problems! Looking for files, moving to get documents, and organizing themselves to do the next task — none of that adds value. Yet not doing these things keeps them from adding value.

Our challenge is to identify wasted motion, and find ways to remove it, even when that motion seems a necessary part of your work.

Value / Motion Kata

Identifying wasted motion starts with a clear understanding of what it is that is of value to your customers. Begin by looking at the end product or service. To the best of your abilities describe value received from the customers' perspective and in the customers' language. Then check with people who have everyday contact with your customers — Sales, Marketing, Project Management, Product Management, Service, etc. Refine the statement of value from the combined perspectives.

Now, share the statement of value with the people performing the work along with the distinction: motion is only work when it adds to the customers' value. This will get them thinking about working towards doing only that work that produces value with no wasted motions. Encourage them to find ways to make their jobs a little easier through *Quick 'Easy Kaizen.*

Repeat the process for each product or service.

Hansei

What are you learning? What surprised you? What will you do to keep the statements of value current with changing customer expectations? How did staff respond to the statement of value? What about their reaction to your invitation that they make their job easier?

JOURNAL

Small minds want more space.

12

Small minds want more space.

Shigeo Shingo

This lesson reminds me of construction job-sites. The more space there is on the site, the more materials seem to take up that space. Construction managers and site superintendents want lay-down space to keep materials ready for use. But the more space they use, the more non-value-adding work has to be performed. Material inevitably has to be moved multiple times before it is used. Material has to be inventoried so it can be found. Material has to be protected from weather. It has to be protected from theft. The more space we use, the less Lean we are. And as all Lean leaders know, inventory is waste.

At the opposite end is the inner-city construction site that has no lay-down space at all. It certainly is more work to coordinate the availability of material so production is not interrupted. Or is it? Downtown job-sites have far less inventory that is moved, damaged, stored, and tracked. Why would we want more space in the first place?

More space is a physical buffer for the variation that occurs in the production of the project. We don't know when something will be completed by one trade, so we don't know when something else will be started by another trade. We want more space to accommodate this variation in task completion — and with the use of that space we add waste to our operations.

Instead, let's go to the source of that waste — the variation in work completions. By decreasing the variation in the completion of work, we won't need buffering. High reliability of task completion uncomplicates the coordination of material arrivals. The reliability of task completion makes *kanban* possible.

How do you improve reliability? By making and securing reliable promises.

Promise Kata

As usual, we start with ourselves. Begin recording the promises you make to include all elements of the promise along with the characteristics of reliability. Follow this form:

I (performer) promise to do something (conditions of satisfaction) for someone (customer) by some specific time in the future. I have the wherewithal to perform; I have estimated the time it will take; I have allocated that time on my schedule; and I sincerely intend to perform, still acknowledging that the future is uncertain, and I might have to revise my promise or take care of the consequences of not performing to my customer's conditions of satisfaction.

Record at least eight promises you make each day for a week. Repeat the process for the following week by recording the promises others make to you. Capture at least eight promises each day.

Hansei

What are you noticing about your reliability? How did it change over the week you recorded your promises? What impact will reliability have on your work? The work of others? What are you noticing about how you work with others? Are they becoming more reliable for you? What is the connection between reliability and waste in your operations?

JOURNAL

If you don't know why defects are occurring, make some defects.

13

If you don't know why defects are occurring, make some defects.

Shigeo Shingo

Making defects seems to be the antithesis of what we want from our processes and our people. Yet, if defects are occurring and we don't know why, then Dr. Shingo's advice is to make even more defects. Why would he say that?

In *Zero Quality Control*, Shingo describes how quality (the lack of defects) should be built into both the product and process design. The process includes the tools, methods, and instruction selection. We all know that errors will occur because we all make errors. Accepting that errors will inevitably happen, Shingo used successive through-process inspection and *poka yoke*[*] (mistake-proofing) to prevent errors from propagating in the process.

Successive checks during a process results in no after-action inspection, and avoids the costly rework or scrap that goes with finding errors only at the end of a process. That is what Dr. Shingo means when he says "zero quality control." The approach calls for vastly more inspections to take place so that rework and mistakes can be avoided.

For example, you perform a process to disassemble and clean your desktop computer. Along the way you may cause damage, you could put parts together incorrectly, or end up with "extra" parts. Each step you inspect allows you to be ready for the next step. For instance, before opening the case, you make sure the computer is off and unplugged. Before touching any exposed electronics, you check that you have grounded yourself. While removing the graphics or memory cards, you notice the orientation of the cards in their slots. You make a mental note, and this prepares you for reinstalling the cards correctly. If you did not make this note, you may find that you reinstall incorrectly, and you'll have to retrace your steps to determine the cause. This takes excess time, and does not add value.

Successive checking entails looking ahead — to follow-on or anticipate tasks while you perform the task at hand. So where do you start? Shingo says, "make some defects,"and then do a *Good 5-Why*[TM] to identify underlying causes.

---

*See Toolkit: Glossary

Good 5-Why Kata

This routine is one of swarming the defect at the place of the defect and with the people who were present when the defect occurred. Use the *Good 5-Why*^{TM} (see Toolkit) approach to learn about the causes. Investigate how successive checks and mistake-proofing can prevent the errors. Follow that investigation with concerted actions to eliminate the causes.

Do this relentlessly for one or two weeks. Use that time to introduce other managers and supervisors to the routine.

Hansei

What are you learning about the source and prevention of defects? What possibilities do you see for your operations and your customers? How might your learning influence the ambition of your goals?

JOURNAL

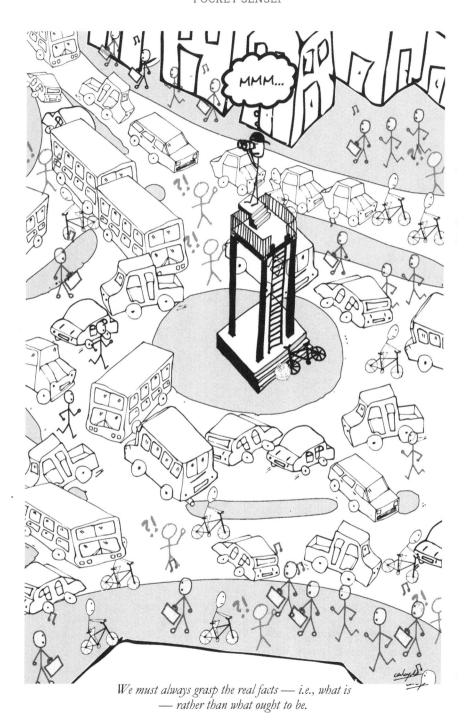

We must always grasp the real facts — i.e., what is — rather than what ought to be.

14

We must always grasp the real facts — i.e., what is — rather than what ought to be.

Shigeo Shingo

Both Dr. Shingo and Taiichi Ohno favored first-hand knowledge of a situation over the reports from others. Some people have interpreted this as not trusting staff. That is not the case. By going to see for oneself at the place of the real work — *gemba* — we are less likely to misunderstand. We are also able to more fully appreciate the nature of the situation. However, there is something more important than understanding the problem — it is understanding the people.

Going to *gemba* to grasp the real facts is one of the most respectful actions leaders and managers can take. When we learn directly from the problems people encounter, we not only learn quicker, but it indicates the seriousness one has for supporting people doing the real work. *Genchi genbutsu* is not just the practice when something has gone wrong — no, "Go and see for yourself" is the way to grasp how different the situation is from the ideal.

I heard Gary Convis at Toyota Georgetown, Kentucky, speak about what he did to make *genchi genbutsu* his daily practice. Gary was the president of Toyota Motors Manufacturing Corp. North America. He could have his office anywhere he wanted in the sprawling Kentucky plant. It could be a corner office with a great view. Not Gary's office. The office could have a waiting area and a receptionist like other company presidents. Not Gary's office. It could be a serene environment with a plush carpet and plush furniture. Not Gary's office.

Gary kept his office in the middle of the production floor. He called it a simple office similar to the production managers' offices. Gary did one other thing to make sure he had the best opportunity to see for himself. He parked his car in a remote area that required him to walk clear across the plant to and from his office — taking him past production areas twice a day at the very least.

For Gary, *genchi genbutsu* wasn't his aspiration. It was designed into his life through the supporting environment he created for himself. Gary's design had him start and finish each day with the important work — the work of seeing for himself. How do you design *genchi genbutsu* into your daily work and habits?

Gary's Office Kata

You are now going to make small changes to your environment and daily routines so *genchi genbutsu* becomes fundamental to what you do daily — not merely an aspiration. You don't need to make radical changes, small changes will do. What can you change about the proximity of your office to the real work? What can you change about how you come and go to work? Can you park so you have to walk the length of the work space? Can you drive to work so you get to go by a project work site daily? Can you schedule your meetings so you have time before or after to walk past and spend time at a production or project setting?

Take time each day for the next two weeks to explore the question, "How can I make my environment and my routines supportive of going to see the work for myself?" Making small changes along the way allows you to evolve your work style into a meaningful, participative, and engaging daily habit.

Hansei

For each change, use the following pages to note what you will change, what effect you thought it would have, what action you took, what result you got and what your learned.

JOURNAL

We must dig up the real cause by asking why, why, why, why, why.

15

We must dig up the real cause by asking why, why, why, why, why.

Taiichi Ohno

Taiichi Ohno is famous for asking five whys. He understood that the root cause was hidden behind the immediate observable causes of problems. By getting to the root cause, problems could be permanently solved.

Ohno called five whys the basis of Toyota's scientific management. The term "scientific management" sprung from the work of Frederick Taylor and his disciples. However, Ohno thought of scientific management differently from the prevailing Western view. At the risk of oversimplifying the idea, the prevailing practice for scientific management was time and motion studies. That was the main practice domain for managers and industrial engineers. This perspective was a clear separation from people performing the work and people planning the work. The Western view placed the emphasis only on management.

Ohno placed his emphasis on the scientist, particularly the practice called the scientific method. His intent was to turn all employees into scientists as they go about their work. To do that, Ohno made a formula to remind people.

$$5 \ Why = 1 \ How^9$$

I made a visit to Toyota's Georgetown, Kentucky, plant with a dozen of my clients to see the factory and meet with Gary Convis, then president of Toyota Motors Manufacturing Corp. North America. Gary said Toyota workers make about 2,000,0000 improvements each year — more than 80% start and finish with a good five why. In other words, five whys is a learning process that will reveal a path for improvement.

Ohno went on to say, "If you can repeat why five times, things will gradually become interesting."[8] How can you train to become good at five whys?

5 Why = 1 How Kata

Identify a very recent small variance, anomaly, or problem that you witnessed. Invite someone who was also present to go with you to the place where that variance occurred. Write down and record your inquiry of the variance. Start by describing the variance clearly and succinctly. Next answer, "Why did that occur?" Record your answer, noting how you verified that it is true. Now answer for the first cause, "Why did that occur?" Continue with the process until you can learn no more. Finish by speculating what actions you can take to eliminate the underlying cause of the variance. Take action to eliminate the cause.

Do this exercise twice a day for a week.

Hansei

What did you learn from the exercise? What was easy? Difficult? What surprised you? What was your partner's experience? What did you notice about your moods throughout the exercise?

JOURNAL

The same as yesterday isn't good enough.

16

The same as yesterday isn't good enough.

Shigeo Shingo

Voltaire said "best is the enemy of better" or "perfect is the enemy of good." Dr. Shingo would agree. But what is "good enough"? Shingo is saying that better today is good enough. I've seen this misinterpreted as "tomorrow will be better than *today*." Yet tomorrow never comes. Make *today* better than yesterday.

Is Shingo calling for "better"? No. He is calling for "different." Do something different today than you did yesterday. Why different? It's not just doing anything differently. That could lead to chaos and anarchy. Shingo wants us to always act with a hypothesis, to use *PDSA* as our personal operating system. When we act with a hypothesis and we do something different, we will learn.

The essence of Lean is learning — learning that is tightly coupled with action. The best way we know to do that is by putting the scientific method to use through *PDSA*.

Managing for learning is the primary role of anyone supervising others. Western culture exalts those who manage for results. Certainly, the majority of US automotive firms have attempted to manage for results. Yet they have been beaten by firms who are managing for learning. To be different today — a little better than yesterday — takes mindfulness. It takes focus to avoid spending all our time on only what is urgent. Better *today* is the important work — the work that we must perform to achieve our ambitions.

Managing for learning works both in the process and the project environments. At the end of projects, many teams reflect with a "lessons learned" practice. People come together to think back on what could have gone better, new things they discovered along the way, and what went well. However, doing "lessons learned" at the end of the project misses the many cumulative opportunities to make the project better every day.

Start each day and every task with the *PDSA* mindset. Choose to make *today* different from yesterday.

New World Kata

Let's return to the practice of starting each day with the important work (*Candy Store Kata*). We will now perform the *kata* by identifying what will be different today from yesterday. Invite someone to work with you to support them making their daily work different. It can be process or project work. Use the *PDSA* approach to define a change, a small change that is performed as an experiment. Use the *PDSA* method to record what the two of you are doing.

Repeat this process throughout the week.

Hansei

What are you learning as you shift your role to manager-as-teacher? What concerns do you have for producing results? What support do you need from others? How are others responding to you? What will it take from you to continue this practice for a week? Month? Year? What will it take from others?

Review your journal entries every few days.

JOURNAL

PART III

Bring others along with you.

Lean requires leadership at all levels. You've been developing your Lean leadership for about two months if you've been doing the *katas* in order. It's time you brought others along with you.

One way to do that is enlist others in a coaching-each-other endeavor. A group of five people offers enough diversity without being so big that each person isn't speaking, or have difficulty in getting others' attention. The people don't need to be committed to Lean full time. Nor do they need to be all at one organizational level. Bring a small group in organization together, from many levels with varying responsibilities.

You also don't need to start at the beginning of the book. This section is a fine place to start. Have everyone practice the same *kata*. With your experience you'll be both an example of open learning for the others and somewhat of a coach.

Keep the coaching-each-other process simple. Meet once a week to share what you are learning, get help from each other, and start a new *kata*. Finish each coaching-each-other session with a *Plus|Delta** to tightly couple your learning with action.

Imagine how much five of you could accomplish for your company, your project, or your customers with this level of concerted self-development.

Bringing others along just might become that tectonic shift.

**See Toolkit: Glossary*

JOURNAL

JOURNAL

Our invariable response to, "It can't be done" is, "Do it!"

17

Our invariable response to, "It can't be done" is, "Do it!"

Henry Ford

Henry Ford's legacy goes far beyond the Ford Production System. It goes beyond the every-man's ownership of an automobile. Ford introduced a way of thinking about harnessing the creativity of the workforce. It was Henry Ford who called for the creation of a process where the Model T took just two days to complete — to go from iron ore to a finished car coming off the end of the line. "Can't be done," you say? Not only was it done, but the River Rouge facility was the exemplary case of mass production and modern management for years thereafter.

We've been involved with a number of impossible goals. Many years ago there was a series of layoffs at the Western Electric plant in the Merrimack Valley in Massachusetts. The Western Electric plant employed tens of thousands of people. Not only was the loss of employment a hit to the economy, there was an even bigger hit in an unexpected place. The Western employees had been big contributors to United Way charities. When thousands of people were suddenly off the payroll, many of those same people now suddenly needed services from United Way agencies. This was a big problem.

The United Way asked other Merrimack Valley firms to increase their giving. Hal volunteered to co-lead the effort at the plant and to participate in the review board for agency funding requests. They were a large factory. Their employee participation hadn't been great. Less than 50% of employees contributed to the charities. They would need nearly 100% participation in giving to have an impact on their community. The company provided a significant match. If they could get 100% it would make a difference. Hal's team set that as a goal. The cries of "It can't be done" followed.

Without going into the details of what they did, they kept our focus on why they were doing it. They reminded people of the great need. They brought agencies in to educate their staff on their specific missions. By bringing everyone's attention to the worthwhileness — "the why" — of the endeavor, "the how" took care of itself. We didn't reach 100%, but we got into the 90% range and the average donation increased.

Lean leaders set impossible goals and then exceed them. How could you learn to do this?

Extreme Why Kata

What would be worthwhile for your organization, project or company? Now make it bigger. How big? Don't let "the how" get in the way of "the why." For instance, Toyota set a goal to reduce repairs under warranty by 80% within a few years. Is it worthwhile? You bet. Did they know how? Not when they started. Word from inside Toyota is that they made good progress. So, let's go back to your situation. What seemingly impossible outcome would be really worthwhile for your customers and your company? Make it big. Share it with others. Get started.

Hansei

As you considered big goals, what did you notice about your internal conversation? Were you getting more ambitious or did you hear yourself say, "Ooh, that's too big"? How much bigger could your goal be if you didn't have to worry about "when"? How much bigger could it be if you weren't worried about "the how"? And how is your concern about failing getting in your way?

JOURNAL

Illusions can easily turn into conventional wisdom.

18

Illusions can easily turn into conventional wisdom.

Taiichi Ohno

Ohno reminds us to critically examine the underlying basis for what we see, read, and hear. When an idea is informed by our preconception, assumption, or interpretation alone, we are always at risk to fully engage with that idea — and to appeal to others' reasoning or participation as well.

David Copperfield, the famous American illusionist, once made the Statue of Liberty disappear in front of a live audience *at the statue*. Of course it was an illusion, but our senses are tricked. If the statue can completely "disappear," what else are we seeing, reading, and hearing that is tricking us?

Crime scene investigators understand that people at the same place, time, and present to the same actions will report different accounts of a situation. The accounts are not fabrications. Each person is giving a sincere impression of what they believe to be true — they are recounting accurately what they witnessed. Yet, their accounts are different.

There is an expression "seeing is believing." It's just not so. The expression is backwards. We see what we believe to be so; we don't see what we don't believe.

Social psychology provides us with a useful concept — Attribution Errors. Superstitions fit this category. Athletes will wear the same article of clothing one game after another, believing that the clothing made for their great performance. The stock market will have a price run-up on the anniversary of some previous price run-up, or in reaction to a recurring public event like a particular team winning a prominent championship.

What we really need is the healthy skepticism of the scientist. The scientist provides the world with a hypothesis, and then proves or disproves that hypothesis. Eventually a prevailing theory is accepted when the hypothesis can no longer be disproved — or — until a challenging hypothesis is introduced again.

As Lean leaders we are continuously confronted with long-held truths (illusions) about how to run, manage, and lead operations or organizations. Is inventory an asset or a waste? Is it better to follow a fixed course, or have the team re-plan as they go? Do you start on the project early if you want to finish on time or do you first go slow so you can go fast later? Contradictions and illusions are significant barriers to progress. Learn to recognize them, and replace them.

Scientific Kata

Start with examining your collective commonsense. What is it that everyone knows to be true, yet someone or some company is doing the opposite? Write that down — let's call this your hypothesis. How do you know it is true? How could the opposite be true? What would you have to see to validate one of the counter hypotheses?

Next, take another look at the hypothesis you wrote down — what experiments could you do?

What is it that you hold to be true that you haven't examined? Where could you look for contrary evidence? Who could you speak with that might have a different experience? What would you need to see to disprove your belief?

Hansei

What are you thinking now about your surety? Hal's wife's Uncle Len used to say, "That might be so," in response to a contrary view to his own. Try reflecting on your hypothesis with Uncle Len's statement.

JOURNAL

*Distinguish between movement and work
to cultivate the ability to find waste.*

19

Distinguish between movement and work to cultivate the ability to find waste.

Taiichi Ohno

By now you might be saying, "Enough already! I get it. Why are we repeating Taiichi Ohno's lesson?"

In our experience, we take for granted that what we are doing is necessary to produce value for the customer. We don't notice the difficulties in performing our work. It is usual to bend or reach to get something. It is usual to take a few moments to position something before working on it. It is usual to uncrate or unwrap items before going to work. Usual, yes. Work, no. Just wasted motion.

Ohno wants us to cultivate the ability to find waste. It's the *finding ability* that is lacking. He says that by making good distinctions between movement and work, we will be better able to find waste. His lesson is itself a *kata*. Make the opportunity to practice that. Do it where you've done the work before. Do it when you think you know everything about the work already. Do it even after you see waste everywhere.

This is like playing scales on a musical instrument. Scales are not music. Practicing scales cultivates the ability to play music. It is an action that prepares us for future action. That is what Ohno wants — that we are ready to find waste. We need to cultivate our ability through playing at finding wasted motion.

You don't need to be at your work to cultivate your ability to see (find) waste. You can do it everywhere you go. You can do it in the kitchen, doing the laundry, working in the garage, and mowing the lawn. You can do it at a sandwich shop and the pizza parlor. Let's take Ohno very seriously.

Look for wasted movement in all work you encounter.

Motion / Work Kata

Go to *gemba* for some time in an *Ohno Circle*. It can be any workplace. Try a construction job-site, a sandwich shop, an engineer's or software developer's office, a tire store, or a garden center. Bring a notepad. Watch people go about their day. At first, they will notice you. They may adjust their behavior to please you. Eventually, you will disappear for them.

Watch movements. Identify a movement that doesn't advance the value for the customers. Record the work step or action, the wasted motion, and the type of waste from *Ohno's 7 Wastes*. Continue the practice until you identify 30 wasted movements.

Repeat this *kata* five times and as often as necessary for a fully cultivated ability.

Hansei

Following each session, note what you are noticing that you haven't noticed before. If you are visiting an unfamiliar business, what did you learn that you can bring back to your business? What action will you take in your business?

After five times, review the notes of the five sessions to make assessments of what you are learning from the first session through the fifth session. What have you learned? What are you getting good at? What needs more of your attention? How will this new skill matter to you as a Lean leader?

JOURNAL

The greatest waste is the waste we don't see.

20

The greatest waste is the waste we don't see.

Shigeo Shingo

Long after Taiichi Ohno named his *7 Wastes,* he added the waste of not using the talents and creativity of the workforce. It's often called the *8th Waste.*[*] It is a waste that you cannot see. Toyota changed dramatically when Ohno renamed "inventory" from an asset to a waste. Toyota changed dramatically again when Ohno named "unused employee potential" a waste. As a result, Toyota is best characterized today as a learning organization that happens to be designing and manufacturing automobiles.

Dr. Shingo's quote above was not about the waste of human potential nor their untapped creativity. However, it is exactly recognizing that waste — Ohno's *8th Waste* — that puts us in the best position to see and then reveal for others the wastes that otherwise would go unseen.

Every time we introduce small group improvement activities or group problem-solving, we see a flurry of improvements made to eliminate waste that had gone unseen — perhaps unseen for years. There was a construction project in Midwest United States where trades people were trained on *Quick 'n Easy Kaizen.* In a matter of a few weeks a group of 30 people were recording 60 or more adopted improvements each month. They were eliminating all that waste with little to no direction from supervision, no investment in tools or equipment, and no slow-down in their productivity. These people were transformed from just project labor to an army of creative waste investigators and eliminators. Months later, that army swelled to over 100 people who improved the construction project at a rate of over 150 adopted improvements per month.

If you agree with Shingo that the greatest wastes are the ones that go unnoticed, then take up the two-fold challenge to eliminate Ohno's *8th Waste* as the vehicle for creating a work environment that thrives on creatively identifying and eliminating the other *7 Wastes* on your projects or processes.

See Toolkit: Glossary

8th Waste Kata

This is not a lesson on mastering *kaizen.*
Volume Two takes up that subject. In this
volume, our focus is on producing Lean
leadership for you and in your organizations
and projects. This *kata* is for seeing waste
that has previously gone unnoticed.

You will need a partner. Choose someone
who is open to examining his or her own
work with you. Spend some time observing
what the person is doing. Look for small
ways that the work could be safer, easier,
or more interesting for the person. Explore
that with the person using questions.
Record your conversation using this
format:

- I had this problem. Describe.
- I made this change. What change?
- It got a little better. What improved?

Repeat this exercise with other learning
partners each morning and afternoon.

Hansei

Notice how you were received by the worker
or colleague. What was their mood? What
was your mood? How did the conversation
go? What did both of you learn? Were you
able to uncover a waste that the two of you
could immediately eliminate? What were
your moods at the end of the session?

See Toolkit: Glossary: Quick and Easy Kaizen

JOURNAL

Before anything else, give it a try.

21

Before anything else, give it a try.

Shigeo Shingo

Experimentation for the purpose of learning is the essence of Lean. The roots of Lean learning can be traced to Sakichi Toyoda's experimentation with automatic looms. But it was W. Edwards Deming that taught the Japanese the *kata* he called *Plan-Do-Study-Act (PDSA)*.[10]

Both Deming and Dr. Shingo made it their point to always operate with a hypothesis. In Deming's *PDSA* language, the *Plan* is the hypothesis. Shingo advises us to move quickly from hypothesis to action by way of doing an experiment.

Shingo doesn't want us to delay our learning by studying the hypothesis. That would be working out of order. Instead, Shingo makes it clear that we only learn when we are in action. Consequently, we want to move quickly from *Plan* (hypothesis) to *Action*. We want to learn — before anything else.

Dr. Shingo is neither naive nor hasty. He did not recommend that we take a grand action. Instead, he is suggesting that we take just that action that will allow us to test our hypothesis. In other words, do *small* experiments. Do experiments in low-risk situations. Do experiments for learning. Do experiments to test ideas.

"Giving it a try" is both a practice and a predisposition to take action that we call "mood." What does it take for you to try something new? What does it take for people around you to try something new? How sure do you and others need to be of success before you give it a try? How concerned are you about how you will look in the face of failure? What is all of this costing you in terms of learning, improving, and excelling at what you and others do?

Let's give it a try!

PDSA Kata

Identify an opportunity to learn from giving it a try. What will your group do today to test your hypothesis that something will be safer, easier, or more interesting? It doesn't have to be big. Small wins add up to big gains. Follow this practice:

Plan: I think _____ will improve when we change _____.

Do: Carry out the change as you described it. Pay attention to your actions and the conditions as you perform.

Study: Were you able to do what you set out to do? Did you get the expected improvement? Why or why not? What do you now know about your ability to perform?

Act: What needs adjustment? What can you now preserve as part of your new standard for performing the work? Who will take those actions? When?

Repeat the process. Give it another try!

Hansei

How confident were you going into your experiment? How confident were others? What were their concerns? What did you notice about your moods as you made tries? What did you learn about yourself? Others? What will you do to make the personal shift towards *PDSA*? Who can you call on for help?

JOURNAL

We must exhaustively pursue our true objectives —
the abstract objects lying beyond what is visible.

22

We must exhaustively pursue our true objectives — the abstract objects lying beyond what is visible.

Shigeo Shingo

Shigeo Shingo had the reputation as an engineer's engineer — an inventor, a mentor, and a visionary pursuing what others deemed impossible.

Dr. Shingo worked at Toyota when the company pursued one big goal after another. One big goal was to catch up with American car manufacturing productivity. Toyota's studies revealed that Ford was ten times as productive as Toyota.[11] Toyota set a goal to catch Ford in three years — and then they did it.[9]

Toyota's early US car exports were of such poor quality that cars were returned to Japan. However, a few years later, their product quality improved so dramatically that Toyota re-entered the US market. Today, Toyota remains a global competitor, ranking first in market value in 2017, followed closely by Tesla Motors.[12]

Toyota set another goal: to reduce repairs under warranty by 80%. Simultaneously, Toyota set a goal of net positive environmental impact everywhere they did business. This led to a near complete elimination of disposable packaging materials for all incoming manufacturing line parts. It also resulted in nearly zero landfill waste. Nothing goes into cafeterias that won't be eaten or end up in their compost pile.

These goals demonstrate the extraordinary results when a group keeps focus on "true objectives." Toyota formalized their planning process on appropriate goals and goal deployment tactics — where the entire organization has opportunity to shape internal objectives and roles towards goals that matter most. The process is called *hoshin kanri* — described as "policy deployment" or top-down bottom-up planning.

Dr. Shingo instructs us to keep our entire organization's attention on what will really matter for the success of our business in the long term.

What Matters Kata

This routine is simple. Ask, "What matters?" Have an answer. Share your answer. Ask others for their answer. Listen openly for something altogether different from what you say matters. Begin crafting with others more powerful answers. Do this relentlessly for at least one week. Then, examine how you and your team are spending your time. Redirect your priorities to match what matters.

Repeat the process with a different group or at a different level of the company. Do it as often as needed to focus attention.

Hansei

What happened while living in that question for a week? What did you learn? What surprised you? What did you have to do to keep that question alive for yourself and for others?

JOURNAL

Rationalize your operation when business is booming.

23

Rationalize your operation when business is booming.

Taiichi Ohno

Rationalize, in today's vernacular, means "justify" or "explain." Engineer Ohno always had a focus on doing only what was necessary to produce a product that was valuable to the customer. All else Ohno deemed waste. Through his work, he identified *7 Wastes* in operations.

In good times it may seem that we have enough sales to justify keeping a little extra inventory. In good times we think that one or two extra people is a small price to pay for flexibility. In good times we don't chase the customer receivable that is two days overdue. In hard times, however, we would do just the opposite — scrambling to meet demands.

Ohno encourages us to always justify what we are doing and to maintain the habit of driving out waste — during good times as well as during bad times. To "rationalize the operation" is a far less daunting task than rationalizing the entire factory, project structure, or design center. What does he mean with "rationalize"? Through what lens do we justify our operations? What is an "operation"?

An "operation" is a step in a process that adds value for the customer. Laying a brick, installing a window, machining a part, assembling a system, writing software sub-proposal or performing a dress-rehearsal before a concert, are all value-adding operations. To rationalize the operation, you have to look at your process through the eyes of the customer. Ask yourself: "Is each step or action producing value for the customer?"

Good Times Kata

Pick a personal "operation" that you repeat at least monthly. The operation might be creating a report, updating a projection, reviewing progress on a project, etc. Note that none of the items we just mentioned produce value unless a customer is paying you to perform the operation. Still, stick with a personal operation.

Map the steps you take to perform the operation. Once mapped, note whether the step adds value or is one of *Ohno's 7 Wastes*. For instance, you might need to run a multi-step calculation repeatedly. To do that you have to look up data that you have used before. While the calculation adds value, the "look-up" is repeated each time you perform the calculation. How about characterizing it as "Unnecessary Movement"? What shortcut or improvement could you make to speed up the operation the next time you perform it?

Continue the mapping until you have described the whole process and have characterized all steps as value or non-value.

Hansei

What did you notice? Was this easy? Or not so easy? Why do you say that? What did you learn about the way you work from the mapping and characterization?

JOURNAL

The medicine won't work unless you take it.

24

The medicine won't work unless you take it.

Shigeo Shingo

Writing this book and any that will follow takes discipline in writing. It's not a discipline Hal had. In fact, in the months leading up to his writing, he stopped blogging. He's been blogging for almost nine years. How is it that he stopped? How could he consider himself a writer if he wasn't writing at least five times each week? The medicine wouldn't work if Hal didn't take it.

Hal resolved to write early each weekday morning before he began work. He started getting up early so he could get in a good two writing hours. Some days it worked. Other times, Hal had gone to bed too late the night before to have much time available in the morning. He wasn't making room in the evenings so he would be fresh to write in the morning.

Writing, or should we say learning to be a writer, is a work-in-progress. Hal needed to remind himself that nothing will get published if he didn't acquire the skills and habits for doing so. The same is true for those of us who intend to be Lean leaders. We must make the time for the important work of learning, practice, and leading. We will never be the Lean leader if we let urgent matters crowd our day. We will never be effective as Lean leaders if we don't stop doing those things that get in the way of learning, practice and leading.

The medicine won't work if you don't take it. Produce a supportive environment so that it is easy for you to take your daily medicine.

Multivitamin Kata

The "medicine" for Lean leaders is learning, practice, and leadership. It is the important work we do each day. Without doing that work you won't become Lean leaders. Begin to introduce a new routine that will support you in attending to the important work.

Start by defining the important work for this day. Start each day with a clear set of actions that you will take to do important work today. Schedule some of that work at the beginning of the day when possible. If you have to come in early for a while to do that, then make it happen. Throughout the day, make quick notes to yourself about what you are noticing when you do the important work. At the end of the day, take a few minutes to reflect on the day's work, make assessments about what you learned, and to write a few notes in this book or your journal. Finish by identifying the important work that you will do tomorrow.

This is *PDSA* in action. Do this daily until it is your habit.

Hansei

Make notes to yourself each day about what was easy and difficult for you that day. Also record what you are learning and what you found surprising. Pay attention to your mood and the mood of those around you. Are you falling into good moods or bad moods? How is that affecting others? What might you do to get your important work done each day?

JOURNAL

JOURNAL

PART IV

Bring focus to all your efforts.

Toyota pursues *flow* as a focusing process for continuous improvement. Of course, improvements in *flow* in itself are good for customers, staff, and the company. With *flow* come lower costs, higher quality, shorter response times, and safer operations. But Toyota doesn't pursue *flow* for those reasons. They pursue *flow* to develop their people. This is the second of *The Toyota Way*[11] principles:

> *Create a continuous process flow to bring problems to the surface.*

The Lean Kanban community (professional services and software companies) understands the power of improving *flow*. They contend all professional services firms have the same three common purposes which they call agendas: (1) to sustainably use the resources of the firm, principally people; (2) to service the customers in a way that meets their needs and the promises that the firm has made; (3) to care for the survival of the firm by providing necessary profits and anticipating and adapting to changes in the market.[13] The Lean Kanban community has a focusing expression:

> *Stop starting, start finishing.*

This focusing statement limits the work-in-process which in turn improves *flow* and shortens the cycle time and lead time. Along the way, quality improves with costs. All are accomplished through continuous improvement. The authors of *This Is Lean*[14] put it this way:

> *The continuously flow-improving organization will always be developing new knowledge, new understanding, new experiences, and learning new things about its customers' needs and how to meet those needs as efficiently as possible.*

What will you do to bring a focus to you and your colleagues over the next eight *kata*s? What focusing declaration will you make?

JOURNAL

JOURNAL

*We will not be able to blaze new trails unless we boldly turn our
thinking processes upside down, and unless everyone participates in that revolution.*

25

We will not be able to blaze new trails unless we boldly turn our thinking processes upside down, and unless everyone participates in that revolution.

Taiichi Ohno

Our common sense gets us through our everyday and every-moment activities. Our accumulated learning allows us to act without thinking. What we call common sense is a fundamental coping mechanism in life. Yet, it is just that kind of non-thinking that keeps us from achieving our desired results.

Taiichi Ohno invites us to engage our thinking in not-so-common ways — upside down — or by recognizing in the moment that our usual ways of coping and navigating are likely insufficient when blazing new trails.

Thinking, Ohno indicates, is a collective endeavor. Our Lean journey requires everyone to reconsider what they know, how they know it, and what will work in a situation. Ohno says we must turn our thinking processes upside down. How can we do that?

The trick is to start with the end in mind rather than the idea. The usual practice is to have an idea and then go shop that idea — the solution in search of a problem. Instead, do as Stephen Covey and Ohno recommend, start with the end in mind. Toyota calls it *hoshin kanri* — strategy deployment. It's the act of getting everyone focused on and committed to a truly worthwhile outcome — a future so different from the present that current ways of thinking become obsolete. The good ideas and thinking will follow.

One way to start is by setting unreasonable goals. What if we had an 80% reduction in transportation? Or a 50% improvement in customer satisfaction — or completely eliminated after-action quality control?

Current thinking is insufficient for achieving bold goals.

Mars Kata

Starting with the end in mind, what is it that if you had more of it, or less of it, would positively change your business, process, or project? Be clear about that. Now, write out the impossibilities that — if possible — would allow you to achieve your ends. Make the list as long as you can make it.

Next, share the ends with others and invite them to make the goals even more unreasonable. One by one, explore how you can turn each impossibility into reality. Do this to challenge your thinking and problem-solving processes.

Repeat the exercise for another unreasonable end.

Hansei

What did you notice about your mood while you did the exercise? What about others' moods? What did you learn about the obstacles or opportunities? What will it take for you to make behavior an everyday practice?

JOURNAL

We use checklists so not to forget that we have forgotten.

26

We use checklists so not to forget that we have forgotten.

Shigeo Shingo

Checklists save lives. They do. A few years ago, patients would go to the hospital for an operation for a left knee and the doctor would operate on the right knee. A few years ago, medical staff would perform surgery and release the patient only to later discover that, when the body responded to an infection, someone had left a sponge behind! A few years ago, patients were more likely to acquire a MRSA infection in a hospital than in everyday life.* What has changed from a few years ago to now?

Checklists. That's right — checklists. Today, medical staff at the best hospitals use checklists to ensure that they remember what they have learned. This is particularly important in repetitive situations. It is in these situations that we fall asleep — we get lazy — mistakes ensue. Patient safety depends on people who remember what they know.

In the 1930's, aeronautics checklists were introduced in response to a crash involving Boeing's newest bomber, model 299, later named the B-17. Following the crash, the plane was characterized as "too much airplane for one man to fly." Rather than redesigning the control system, test pilots introduced simple short checklists for takeoff, flight, landing, and taxiing. The checklists worked. The US military ordered thousands of B-17's.[15]

Dr. Shingo reminds us forgetfulness is part of our human condition. Not that we forget forever. We think that because we *can* remember that we *will* remember. Yet, we all know that even a small distraction is enough for us to forget for the moment.

Checklists are generally valuable in four situations: when the person is inexperienced; when the operation is performed infrequently; when present to distractions; and when there are significant negative consequences from performing improperly. Routine, repetitive and mind-numbing work is all around us. It can directly lead to an error that endangers us and others.

* Methicillin-resistant Staphylococcus aureus (MRSA) is a bacterial infection that is highly resistant to some antibiotics.

Parachute Kata

We can't use checklists without making them. Pick a task with some complication to it. Refresh your memory of the steps by performing the task. Once completed, write out the important steps. When satisfied that you have them all, go back to the beginning to identify and record for each step any points of attention. When satisfied, attempt to perform the task again by following your checklist. Make any necessary corrections to the checklist so it represents successful completion of the task.

Hansei

Producing good checklists takes practice. The *kata* is not intended to produce checklist competence. Rather, the *kata* is about producing an appreciation for the value of employing checklists in your work and the work of others. What was your experience producing checklists? What about using your checklists? How was value produced for you?

JOURNAL

Find problems where you think none exist.

27

Find problems where you think none exist.

Shigeo Shingo

Shouldn't we be spending most of our time where the problems are? Dr. Shingo seems to be countering the common sense axiom "If it ain't broke, then don't fix it." Could Dr. Shingo be looking for trouble where none exists?

Dr. Shingo has shown us that our common senses are full of illusions — especially when we are dealing with the everyday activities. When something is working well, we tend to accept it as a common sense standard, and then we risk becoming so complacent that we miss opportunities for great advancement.

It is easy to get complacent when all seems fine — especially in the workplace. Complacency leads to boredom, which leads to resignation. Complacent team members stop looking and stop thinking. Innovation will not happen if thinking doesn't happen.

Finding problems among the best operations keeps the people in those operations engaged and challenged. How do we do that? Many companies only measure outcomes. How many did we ship? How good was the final product? How much did it cost us? How many items were scrapped? What rework was required? These are all outcome measurements. Lean companies have these measures, but the measures they pay closest attention to are the process measures.

Let's say that we are drilling a ¼" hole ½" deep in a metal block. What variables might contribute to getting a clean hole matching the specification every time? Some variables to consider are drill speed, bit sharpness, drill pressure, axial rotation, machine vibration, etc. Each of these variables can be measured. For instance, a slower drill speed could lead to a bad hole. Or, not maintaining pressure could lead to excessive time to drill the hole. Or, machine vibration could result in a hole that was slightly oversized.

The same thing applies to knowledge or project work. What are the variables in your project work? How often are tasks ready to be started and completed according to the plan? Are you keeping project performers current with changes to the plan? Are performers promising task completion in reliable ways? These are some of the variables that bring about good project outcomes. Track variables to find unnoticed problems.

Variable Kata

Pick a good operation. Identify the process variables. What conditions must be maintained to continue to make a good product? Establish upper and lower targets of acceptability. Then track the variables either through continuous monitoring or statistical sampling. Engage a process quality specialist to understand appropriate approaches. Look to learn from this. What variances do you see that lead to poor outcomes?

Repeat this for a number of your good processes.

Hansei

What are you learning about your operations? Are you finding new problems? Are they leading to process improvements? What are the reactions from the work-group? Are they more interested in continuous improvement? Where else might you benefit from this approach?

JOURNAL

Everyone confuses motion with work.

28

Everyone confuses motion with work.

Taiichi Ohno

One hot summer day, Hal and his three sons were moving sand in their yard. They were preparing the ground for a paver stone patio. Along the way, one son noticed that they had over-excavated an area. Surely, the four of them were working hard, their sweat-soaked bodies were evidence. But they expended their effort without advancing their cause. In fact, they created the situation where they would have to expend more effort to restore the over-excavated area.

Taiichi Ohno reminds us to observe all action (motion) so that we can assess whether or not it is advancing our goals. Are the actions adding the intended value, or are the actions — or parts of the actions — needlessly expending energy? It is easy to think we are working when we are not clear about what value we are producing. In Hal's family situation, they kept moving sand without attention to the depth they actually needed. They were well-meaning. They were chatting it up enjoying their time together. They certainly toiled in the hot sun. But it was not work (according to Ohno) — merely motion.

Most people in the work setting are in motion. But is that motion focused on an outcome that customers would call value? If not, then we can't call it work — we can only call it labor. We avoid the confusion between work and motion when we have the customer's perspective of value while we perform the work.

The first Lean Thinking principle is to establish what is of value to the customer from the customer's perspective and in the customer's language.[16] When you keep that value in mind, you will avoid the confusion.

Stop / Motion Kata

All workers — people who exercise motion for the sake of producing value — need to know exactly what conditions will be assessed as value by a customer. The customer can be internal or external. Often the customer is not present. The customer might not be known.

Start with your own work. Pick something that you do. Who is the customer for that? What outcome or conditions will satisfy the customer? How do you know? Speak with your customer to confirm your conclusions.

Now, examine your work. Are you performing just those actions (motions) that will produce your customer's conditions of satisfaction? If not, then stop doing those actions. Are there conditions of satisfaction that you are not meeting? Change your work to satisfy your customer.

Repeat the process on different tasks each day of the week.

Hansei

Make notes about how easy or difficult it was to identify your customer and what is valuable. Also reflect on how changes to your work affected your mood. Could you stay mindful of the customer's conditions of satisfaction while you performed your work? What got in your way? What will you try next time to be more mindful?

JOURNAL

Usually mass production raises costs.

29

Usually mass production raises costs.

Taiichi Ohno

How can mass production raise costs? Economies of scale is a fundamental principle taught in any economics course. The idea that increasing volume brings decreasing costs is behind the cost reductions in the semiconductor business for the past 40 years. There's even a name for it — Moore's Law. It turns out that Moore's Law is an anomaly.

Mass production is generally understood to mean optimizing operations for volume production. A way to understand this is to look at various parts in a car.

One supplier makes water pumps. The supplier has calculated that the optimum production run for a water pump in their factory is 10,000 units. Each car gets one pump. But cars have other parts too. How about serpentine belts? Another producer might determine the optimum quantity for a production run is 15,000 belts. Alternators are produced by a third company, who decided their optimum is 8,000 units before switching over to another car model. The volumes between the three companies are not matched. The unmatched quantities add costs for the auto assembler — storage, handling and ordering processes — all costs that add to cost of the assembly process but add no value to the auto itself or for the customer of the auto.

Ohno advocates to make just those parts that you need to produce the cars that will be sold and built. Anything else is over production — one of *Ohno's 7 Wastes*. Producing only for what's needed eliminates the extra handling, storage, record-keeping and ordering processes.

Unit-of-one production or single-piece *flow* is the approach for fulfilling Ohno's direction to "make only what you can sell."

Change-over Kata

How do we break our illusionary addiction of the value of mass production? Start by cutting production runs in half. We also did this in *Pie Kata*. But now, cut all your production runs in half. All batch sizes. All planning durations for all project-based work. But not all at once. You need a plan.

Use the *A3 Format* for planning an initiative. List all the major production runs. Order them from highest to lowest by run quantity.

Pick one operation or one batch that you will cut in half. Closely watch the process to discover what difficulties arise. You will usually see the difficulties in the set-up or changeover steps to move from one batch to the next. But maybe not. Maybe changeover only takes a few minutes. If so, cut the batch in half again. If not, first go to work on cutting the changeover by at least half.

Repeat the exercise for the same item before moving on to the next largest batch on the list.

Hansei

Notice your reaction to the boldness of the action. Did you think it was unreasonable? Achievable? What about the people performing the process? What did you need to do to gain their support and involvement? Are you ready to do it again on the same process? Different process?

JOURNAL

*The best way to clean something is to make sure
it doesn't get dirty in the first place.*

30

The best way to clean something is to make sure it doesn't get dirty in the first place.

Shigeo Shingo

There is a practice on some projects in the commercial construction industry of having each trade contractor contributing one or more staff to a Thursday afternoon clean-up crew. Debris accumulates through the course of the week, aisles get clogged, dirt gets into places it is not intended to be, and the site is less safe than it would be if it were clean. Cleaning up doesn't add any value to the project from the customer's perspective. Yet without cleaning up the customer may not get all that was promised.

Some contractors maintain a clean-as-you-go policy. This avoids the big weekly clean-up exercises. But clean-as-you-go is still cleaning up. Wouldn't it be better to work in a way that the workspace doesn't get dirty? Of course it would. But when Hal says that to construction people he gets a stern look and then a lecture on how construction waste is just part of the process. On one occasion he was accused of being very new to the business.

But what if Dr. Shingo is right? Can we work in ways that the work setting doesn't get dirty? Not only can we, but it is safer and cheaper to do so. A year or so ago, Hal visited a manufactured building operation. When he stepped into the plant his eyes immediately began to water from the dust in the air. "You'll get used to it," he was told. The dust was created from cutting rock-faced plastic sheeting used to sheath buildings. The workers cutting the material were wearing respirators but that didn't keep the dust from making its way to everyone else and to the corners and crevices of the buildings. Everything had to be cleaned throughout the process and again before packaging and shipping. The situation was easily remedied with a vacuum dust collection system. And with it, all the cleaning went away.

Work in such a way so that you don't create something that has to be cleaned later is an attitude — a waste-eliminating principle.

Cleaning is waste.

Ship-shape Kata

Follow this routine: pick an area that is being cleaned on a regular basis. What small experiment could you do with your associates in that area to keep the operation area from getting dirty at all? (Remember, clean-as-you-go is still cleaning, and cleaning is still wasteful.) How might that affect the quality of that product or other products? How might you make changes that are low cost or no cost to adopt? Write this out and work it out. Enroll the people who do the work to do the experiment. Evaluate the results. Make adjustments. Do the experiment again, and again.

Alternative routine: pick an area that is dirty but is not being cleaned.

Hansei

Why do you suppose that you and others have accepted cleaning in your operations? Now that you see it as waste, what will it take from you to change your attitude into action? How have your associates responded to your new view of the situation? What have you noticed about your mood and their moods? What will it take for you and your staff to continue with this practice?

JOURNAL

Stand on the production floor all day and watch —
eventually you will discover what has to be done.

31

Stand on the production floor all day and watch — eventually you will discover what has to be done.

Taiichi Ohno

Taiichi Ohno is said to have told staff to "stand in a circle" at *gemba* — the place of the real work — to identify wastes. The *Ohno Circle* is the name that people use for the practice of standing in one spot to see what is going on and to identify waste.

The *Ohno Circle* is just one example of *genchi genbutsu* — go and see for yourself. It is as important today to Toyota as it was when Engineer Ohno was walking the manufacturing floor.

Hal first experienced *genchi genbutsu* at a design-build construction company in the late 1990s. He had conducted a number of *Study-Action Teams*™* using the book *Lean Thinking*.[16] The principal architect got very curious and started reading Ohno's books.

After spending three hours sitting 50 yards from the job-site on a "pile of waste" (as he affectionately called the site inventory), the architect came to see Hal. He showed him dozens of pages filled with notes that he made about the waste he saw from just a single vantage point.

His observations and assessments from those three hours created a stir among the managers. His notepad full of waste observations led to weeks of improvement activities. Up until then, they had been reading, studying, and experimenting with Lean practices. They could claim to have a "little Lean this" and a "little Lean that" happening on numerous construction projects and in the design studio. But they weren't taking the time at *gemba* to observe for themselves what was adding value for their clients — and what was waste. Nor were they taking the time to help people eliminate the waste that was found.

How do you start this practice? How do you find opportunities at *gemba*?

See Toolkit: Glossary.

30 Min Gemba Kata

There are a number of *Ohno Circle* approaches, but the best we've found comes from Jon Miller, author of the Gemba Panta Rei[17] blog. In "Give Me 60 Minutes and I'll Give You a Lean Transformation," Jon provides the following exercise:

> *"You'll need a piece of paper with 30 or more lines on it. You'll need something to write with. You might need something to put the paper on and write against. This exercise starts with picking a spot in your gemba and standing in that one place for 30 minutes. Find 30 things to improve in 30 minutes. Write them down.*

> *"Take the next 30 minutes and make at least one of the improvements you wrote down. The other improvements you can spend the rest of the month working on bit by bit, delegating to the appropriate people, or asking people 'why' until you find the actionable root cause."*

Take the exercise seriously. Work with the people in the area you observed for the three weeks, knocking off two or three improvements each day. As Jon Miller says, if you and the other managers do this it will produce a Lean transformation.

Hansei

Make notes after standing in a circle and each day following the improvements you made. What was easy? What was challenging? How did the work-group respond to you? What did you notice about your moods?

JOURNAL

All our knowledge and understanding won't get us
anywhere unless we are able to act on it.

32

All our knowledge and understanding won't get us anywhere unless we are able to act on it.

Shigeo Shingo

We are reminded of a young man working for a stone mason. A short time ago he learned about Toyota's A3 problem-solving approach. He wasted no time looking for the right problem to solve. He didn't delay while reading more about the A3 approach. He didn't ask his manager for permission to proceed. Instead, this young man looked for the first problem he could find to begin his process of learning A3 Thinking.

Dr. Shingo teaches us to get into action so we have the opportunity to learn. Learning happens when we are in action. Sure, we can learn *about* something without being in action, but learning to *do* something always requires doing something.

That young man is Hal's son. He did his first *first-run study** without ever having seen one. Where did he find this enthusiasm, bravery, or confidence to simply act on something he's never done before? He felt this way because he trusted that he would not suffer from looking bad in front of his manager if he tried something that didn't quite work. That trust was built through a series of trials. He learned; the team learned — and his manager appreciated the learning efforts. He did his first *Good 5-Why*™ root-cause analysis after a brief phone introduction. He learned. The team learned. His manager appreciated their efforts.

Becoming able to act on new knowledge — and developing proficiency — first requires a work environment that encourages learning before expecting results. It's not so difficult. It's about emphasis, attention, and enthusiasm.

Encourage your teams to learn and then appreciate their efforts.

See Toolkit: Glossary

Laboratory Kata

The lesson here is to support people in making their tries. First tries are often the most challenging. We are often so worried about looking bad, that we don't try those things that will have us look good. Try this:

Introduce *Quick 'n Easy Kaizen* to a small group. Help each of them come up with a small improvement to their own work. Ask them to come up with another small improvement in the next five days. Each day, spend a little time with one person helping them try something that makes their job a little safer, easier or more interesting. Encourage their actions. Appreciate their efforts. Share the results with the whole group.

Hansei

People are all creative. It doesn't always appear that way. It also doesn't appear that people can learn. Both learning and creativity are supported by the way we engage. How do you engage? How was this *kata* different from your everyday engagement? What did you learn? What was easy for you? What was difficult? What reaction did you get from the small group? What will you do to continue to shape a work environment where people are learning and innovating?

JOURNAL

PART V

Embrace contradictions

By now you've noticed that Lean is full of contradictions.

- Go slow so you can go fast.
- Pursue perfection, yet perfect is the enemy of better.
- Be agreeable while dissatisfied.
- Try something before you say you can't do it.
- Don't focus on resource efficiency, focus on flow efficiency. Doing so will increase resource efficiency.
- Adopt standard work so you can continuously improve.

In the background of many Lean contradictions is a precept to focus on the process not the people (Deming) and "the right process will produce the right results" (Toyota Way). The ultimate extension of that is the claim that Western management fixation on managing for results is shortsighted. Instead, by managing for learning (and improvement) we will achieve far better results.

There's a great story in *This Is Lean* about a Lean expert who served as Taiichi Ohno's second-in-charge.[14] A European engineering company had been on a Lean journey for many years. They invited Ooba-san to visit their facility to assess if they were Lean. He toured the facility, listened to staff, and then spoke with his hosts at the end of the tour. The chairman of the firm asked,

> *"Ooba-san, we have now shown you the whole factory and told you about our work on lean, which we are very proud of. We are wondering now if you consider this to be world-class lean?"*

Ooba-san's answer was short and to the point.

> *"It is impossible for me to say. I wasn't here yesterday."*

Managing for learning and improving — every day, always — rather than managing for results, is the path to Lean. Yes, it flies in the face of what we learned in school, as we learned to supervise, and as we went about our jobs. That it contradicts our common sense only means we need an uncommon sense.

The sooner you embrace the contradictions, the faster you will grow as a Lean leader.

JOURNAL

If we don't understand what it is that we don't understand, we have no idea what to do about it.

33

If we don't understand what it is that we don't understand, we have no idea what to do about it.

Shigeo Shingo

Our blindness to our ignorance is a great hazard. This is as true about our work setting as it is about our personality. We don't have to think about that for very long before we see the perplexity in taking any action to remove the ignorance.

There is a personal discovery tool known as the Johari Window.[18] The window is created as a 2 x 2 matrix using the two characterizations: what is known and what is not known; and two or more observers (self and others). Three quadrants deal with what is known by someone; as Shingo says, they are understandable. It's the fourth quadrant — the unknown, that neither we nor others are able to characterize — that is an enigma and the big opportunity.

What can we do about the unknown? One place to look for some help is the Aspen Institute and the annual TED conference. The Aspen Institute calls it "intellectual inquiry and exchange."[19] At TED they call it "ideas worth sharing."[20] The novelty of both groups is the eclectic melding of personalities, perspectives, professions, and paradigms.

Something new is revealed at the intersection of expertise. What is it that we can do as Lean leaders to move to that space? We can adopt an open stance and an interest in others' interests. The opposite of that is provincialism — where participants in the community provide their own body of knowledge and educate members in that body of knowledge to the exclusion of other influences on that community. The extreme situation is a cloistered religious sect.

"Enlightening" is the characterization we will use for being open and interested in others' interests. It gives us the chance of being enlightened together. The architect in conversation with the anthropologist and entrepreneur come together in a way that resulted in some of the best writing on Lean thinking for the built environment.[21] Construction project managers and government bureaucrats visit Toyota's production facilities for the purpose of being influenced in a new way, to engage in a different interpretation of what they know and don't know about their own operations, and to leave with questions that they never considered.

Engage in enlightening practices.

Mind-field Kata

Read mathematics. Read philosophy. Read *The Economist*. Read *Cosmopolitan*. Read about projects. Read about Korean entrepreneurs. Subscribe to *Harvard Business Review* and to *Fast Company*. Subscribe to *Engineering News Record* and to *Wired*. Watch a TED video once a week for nine months. Talk to people about what you are reading and watching. Visit other businesses. Create a mind-field.

Hansei

Keep a journal recording what you are learning, what opportunities you are seeing and what new questions you are asking Review your journal at least every two weeks to notice how you are engaging differently, how you are opening to the world, and what new interests you have in others' interests.

JOURNAL

"Know-how" alone isn't enough!
You need "know-why!"

34

"Know-how" alone isn't enough! You need to "know-why!"

Shigeo Shingo

Too many companies stop short of helping their staff perform their jobs. They tell people what they want done, but fail to help them to succeed in accomplishing their responsibilities. When asked, staff are usually able to tell you what they are supposed to do — the know-*what* — but they have not been instructed in the know-*how* of their position. This is a failure of supervision.

It is every supervisor's and manager's job to have staff that is able to perform the responsibilities of their positions. In the lead-up to WWII, the US War Department ran a program called *Training Within Industry: Job Instruction.*[22] The program trained supervisors in the basic responsibilities of supervision. A key responsibility was having staff that could perform their functions competently. Even at that time, the instructors understood that knowing what to do and how to do it were insufficient to get good performance over the long term. Staff must understand the know-*why* to perform their jobs at the level that was needed.

Why is know-*why* so important? While the know-*what* might not change, the know-*how* is bound to change in a constantly learning and adaptive organization. Without understanding the know-*why*, staff are likely to introduce changes that will not improve the situation. Or, worse, they will introduce defects or difficulties for others.

The responsibility for know-*why* rests with the manager-as-teacher. However, merely sharing know-*why* is not enough. It needs to be part of staff training and the description of standard work. Know-*why* is the critical job knowledge for every Lean enterprise. It allows the people closest to the work to make improvements without a bureaucracy of management approvals. Organizations with attention to know-*why* are nimbler and improve performance at rates far higher than their competitors. That's Lean.

Standard work and good job instruction are foundations for sustaining know-*why* in the organization. Are they in place in your organization? How can you build a know-*why* culture?

Know-Why Kata

It's now time to go back to *gemba*. This time you are out to learn what people understand or don't understand about why they do what they do. You'll want to bring a mood of curiosity to your questioning to avoid having your intentions be misinterpreted. Use the simple question, "Why do you do that?" to discover the know-*why*. Follow that question with, "How did you learn that?" to see the extent to which people know what they know.

Make this part of your daily visits to *gemba*.

Hansei

What are you learning about the way you have been engaging? Are people receptive to your questioning? Why do you say that? Are you comfortable engaging in these conversations? Are you beginning to look forward to making your daily trip to *gemba*? How is this new practice supporting your shift from managing-for-results (outcomes) to managing-for-learning (process)?

JOURNAL

Understanding alone isn't enough to get people moving.

35

Understanding alone isn't enough to get people moving.

Shigeo Shingo

The US education system puts great emphasis on testing what students know *about*. Hence, we think that know-*about* is what is important rather than being able to perform. Know-*about* is the precursor to know-*how*. But to advance on an everyday basis, we must also have know-*why*.

Let's talk about golf. Someone can tell you about putting in golf. They can describe the process of reading the green, lining up the shot, going through a pre-shot routine, and then putting with a pendulum swing. You will understand some of what a golfer is doing the next time you see one putting. However, unless you too are a golfer, you won't be able to take effective action. Effective action takes practice.

Training Within Industry (TWI)[22] used an approach during WWII for teaching tasks that included showing the important steps, the key points for attention, and the reasons why.[21] Workers not only learned the what and how, they learned why they were doing what they were doing. This created a foundation for ongoing improvement by the people who were trained.

Experimentation, assessment, and reflection develop the know-*why*. A Lean leader validates what is understood and discovers what is not yet understood by getting people moving. Staying in action by continuing *katas*, getting feedback from people who are more competent, by seeing effects, and understanding results, builds proficiency and know-*why*.

Shingo tells us that to reap the rewards of learning or creating new knowledge, we need to get people moving. When we focus on continuous experimentation, we get advances to both the know-*whats* and know-*hows*. It is the virtuous cycle that separates Lean companies from their competitors.

Both Shingo and Ohno learned to put the scientific method in everyday use from Dr. Deming's lessons. Deming called it *Plan-Do-Study-Act*. Getting people in motion is about the *Do*. But, unlike the "don't just stand there, do something" knee-jerk response to an idle worker, Shingo wants you to act based on what you actually know — the *Study* before you *Act*. It is the opportunity to prove or disprove your hypothesis. More simply, you get to learn what you really *don't* know yet.

My Hypothesis Kata

Start each task with a hypothesis of what outcome you will get when you take action in a certain way. Then take that action. Next, evaluate: were you able to act as you intended? If so, did you get the result that you anticipated? If so, then proceed to take action again. If you didn't get the anticipated result, then study what you didn't understand about the situation. Make an adjustment. Now proceed with a new plan (hypothesis).

Do this for four or five tasks each day for a week. Record your observations and thoughts about your learning in your journal. Repeat the process for a second week.

Hansei

What are you noticing about the way you are seeing your work and your world as you practice *PDSA*? What benefits do you speculate you will get as you make *PDSA* your habit? How are other people reacting to your new-found attention on deeply learning from the work you perform? What will it take from you to continue this practice? How will you create a supporting environment for that?

JOURNAL

We act on what we think is true. Don't act on assumptions.

36

We act on what we think is true. Don't act on assumptions.

Shigeo Shingo

People naturally make assumptions about conditions that they have previously observed. Our success at assuming perpetuates the bad habit. Ohno made a similar warning when he said, "Illusions can easily turn into conventional wisdom." Dr. Shingo takes it further: what if the assumptions are simply wrong? Even the assumptions that you have been making with no apparent negative consequences? What are you giving up for the sake of expediency?

Why would Shingo say never act on assumptions? If I just left a situation, can't I assume that it is as I left it? What about having seen the situation yesterday? Two days ago? Two weeks ago? At what point are my facts stale?

We frequently encounter managers who confidently explain how an organization performs their work. We ask, "How do you know?" The usual answer is, "The process was designed that way." Or, "That is the way I trained the staff." Or, "The system only works in this way." I follow, "When did you last look?" [blank stare] "Let's go have a look."

When we act only on our assumptions, we create organizational complacency. In essence, acting only on our assumptions means we don't have to do anything different today than we did yesterday. This is the antithesis of Lean. It is the antithesis of embracing Dr. Deming's *Plan-Do-Study-Act* — the scientific method for everyday work.

The practice of *genchi genbutsu* — going to see for yourself — is the practice to combat the convenience of assuming. At first, it may look impractical to make time to go to *gemba* on existing practices or work routines; however, taking the time to see for yourself will keep you from making mistakes and retaining false or weak assumptions.

Break the bad habit of assumption.

Our Hypothesis Kata

Go to *gemba* as a normal work routine. Write down what you expect to find, and then go look for any deviations from your assumptions. Do it today. Do it in the morning and the afternoon. Do it out of respect for the people you work with and support. Do it tomorrow and the next day. Do it when you hear about successes. Do it when there are errors or variances. Do it for your learning. Write down things you didn't expect to find. Go to *gemba*, ask questions and be ready to answer questions. Be ready to be helpful and challenge your assumptions.

Make notes along the way. Repeat the process.

Hansei

Where in your busy day are you making time to be with the people doing the real — value-adding — work of your organization? How will you do that again tomorrow? And the next day? What help, if any, do you need from others to maintain the practice?

JOURNAL

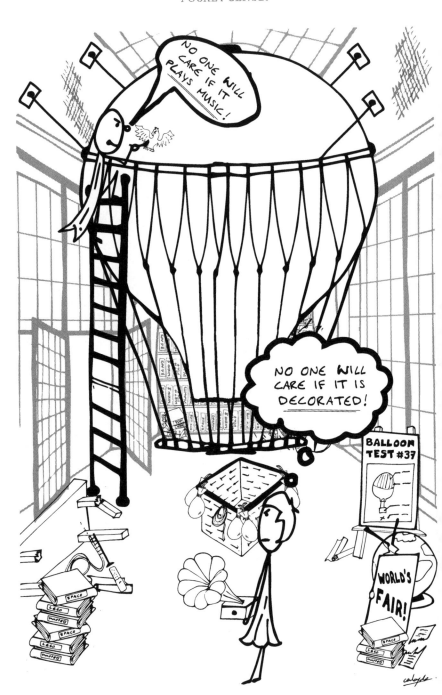

Find waste!

37

Find waste!

Shigeo Shingo

Two words. Just two words, yet those two words can define a life's work. At least it defined Dr. Shigeo Shingo's work. He was tireless in his efforts to rid a system of all waste. And he was clear that first you must find that waste.

We've discussed *Ohno's 7 Wastes* and different versions of the *8th Waste*. Now let's look at two other wastes: the wastes of not speaking and of not listening. We call these the *Two Great Wastes.*[23] *

Early in Hal's work with construction firms he noticed that clients understood *Ohno's 7 Wastes*, but they weren't taking action to investigate these wastes. When variances occurred they didn't do root cause analysis; they didn't act on the Pareto charts they were keeping; they didn't look for ways to make today better than yesterday. We had introduced these approaches, but they didn't do them. Hal got curious as to why. So, he spent time listening at project meetings and walking job-sites and found something very interesting.

Inevitably, the first thing he noticed was the conversation that happened after the meeting. In leaving the meeting, Hal overheard people offering observations, assessments, and speculations about what could be done to address the issues they just finished discussing in the meeting. But they didn't raise those issues in the meeting. During the meeting they sat quietly. The other thing he noticed were that the supervisors, foremen and project managers had their attention exclusively on their agenda or their issues, completely failing to notice what meeting participants were actually saying.

Not speaking and not listening produces stagnation — no progress is possible in the presence of these *Two Great Wastes.*

See Toolkit: Glossary.

Two Great Wastes Kata

This is a two-part exercise. Use your journal to record when you notice you have something to say, but you either failed to say it or you hesitated before saying it. Record the situation: who you were speaking with; the topic; what you were saying; and what you suppose was in your way.

Next, notice those situations where you catch yourself not paying attention to others — specifically where someone was trying to speak or where otherwise engaged people were sitting quietly. Record the situation: who you were speaking with; the topic; what you were saying; and what you suppose you were doing that kept you from listening.

Do this for a few days until you have a dozen or more observations. Look for a pattern in those observations and speculations. Have a conversation with a colleague about what you see and how you might adjust your behavior to create more speaking around you and more listening from you. Continue the exercise as you experiment with your behavior and have a follow-up discussion with a colleague.

Hansei

Could you catch people not speaking in your presence? How about you not listening? How did the conversation go with your colleague? What surprised you in that conversation? How did the first experimentation go? What did you learn about yourself? What did you learn about others?

JOURNAL

"Eliminate waste!" is a nonsensical slogan.

38

"Eliminate waste!" is a nonsensical slogan.

Shigeo Shingo

The first time Hal recalls hearing this statement from Dr. Shingo was in 1987. He was working at Digital Equipment Corp. in Salem, New Hampshire. He just returned from a study mission to Japan with 23 other managers from about ten manufacturing locations. They had prepared themselves for five months reading on *Just-in-Time, Total Quality Management,* and Japanese ways of excelling at manufacturing. None of them had read any of Taiichi Ohno's and Shigeo Shingo's texts yet.

On their return they were tasked to lead improvement activities at their plants, specifically to eliminate waste. It seemed like a reasonable request. All 24 of them enthusiastically agreed. "Eliminate waste!" quickly became one of the favorite poster slogans on their facility walls. But eliminating waste was not easy. Sure, they had been trained in various efficiency practices. Many of them had backgrounds in statistics, process control, design of experiments, or industrial engineering. Yet, they made slow progress to eliminate waste.

Then, one member of the group finally went and read Dr. Shingo's blue book.[24] He discovered that their task wasn't to eliminate waste at all — it was to *find* the waste and learn about its various causes. Once they learned about the sources of variation and waste, the actions would be obvious.

The posters came down. They went about their work differently. They began to see waste everywhere. And they began investigating that waste with the people closest to it. Now, eliminating waste became easy.

Waste Finder Kata

This *kata* is about finding waste. It starts by getting into the habit of looking for it. You've already had experience with the *Ohno Circle*, what else can you do? Jon Miller claims that 60 minutes will result in a transformation. If you and other leaders are already spending the 60 minutes each along with the time to improve 29 other situations, then you've made a great start. The challenge now is to get the whole workforce in the practice of finding waste.

The waste-finding habit is naturally acquired when the focus is personal. What is just a little difficult in your own work? What is uninteresting? What is unsafe? These are areas that already interest you. Use *Quick-n-Easy Kaizen* to make improvements as you see waste in your own work. Keep your attention on the little difficulties — the places where you are bored and the situations that have a possibility for danger. This is how you will enhance your waste-finding skills.

Make a point of helping others notice waste in the same way. Do it one-on-one and in small work-groups. Continue to do this until a critical mass of waste-seeing is in place.

Hansei

Eliminating waste is easy once we see it and study it. What are you learning as you are helping others see and study waste? What is rewarding for you? What are you finding to be difficult for you in helping others? Who might help you with that?

JOURNAL

*When carrying out improvements, you will only be truly effective
when you first set your objectives and then head straight for them.*

39

When carrying out improvements, you will only be truly effective when you first set your objectives and then head straight for them.

Shigeo Shingo

Toyota has a long-standing practice of setting very clear, seemingly unreachable goals — then heading straight for them and exceeding their goals. At the company or business level, the goal-setting process is called *hoshin kanri*. It is a top-down and bottom-up process that establishes the primary direction along with the organizational alignment to pursue and achieve the goal.

Dr. Shingo is famous for setting the objective of performing a changeover activity (or set-up) in single minutes. It didn't matter what the current time was, he would often call for a 90% reduction in the changeover time. And he meant *Now!* Shingo wasn't shy to express his displeasure when the goal wasn't achieved even when the group had a greater than 50% reduction.

The practice at Toyota appears to have been moderated since Shingo's time. Toyota now sets big goals but they are less clear about the time for achieving the goals. We have long-advocated to go for better *now* and repeat the process once better was achieved. This is more consistent with Dr. Deming's *PDSA*[10] approach to learning and improvement.

Setting clear objectives and heading straight for them also works for small groups. Hal was working with a swimming pool company at one of their divisions. They were taking about 120 calendar days to perform just 15 days of physical work. In other words they were taking on average 17 weeks to do just three weeks of work — less than 17% *flow efficient.** That whole time the customer had her backyard torn up. They set a clear goal that all pools would take no more than twice the estimated days to perform the work — an average of six weeks. They were calling for a 65% reduction in the time from dig to swim. Impossible? Seemingly. But not when the local group kept acting on measuring waiting times, delays, mis-coordination, and rework out of the process. In just a few months, they cut the time in half.

We see managers and work-groups avoiding the specificity in their objectives that Shingo calls for. As a result, they get satisfied once they are a little better. Don't let complacency follow achievement. Improve by 50% and then do it again!

**See Toolkit: Glossary*

Improvement Kata

What needs to be improved in your work setting? How much would it have to change for your customer to notice? Meet with the people who work in that area, and then set a goal for a particular improvement. Write it down. Post it prominently. Focus the group on pursuing that goal by making it the important work for every day. Monitor and post the progress you are making.

Once the goal is accomplished, raise the bar!

Hansei

How hard was it for you to set a seemingly unreachable yet very specific objective? What do you suppose has kept you from doing it as your routine? What will you do about it so that those barriers are gone? How have people responded to your cooperative goal-setting? How about your involvement in their success? How has your mood changed? Make notes on the following pages or in your journal.

JOURNAL

Never say, "Impossible."

40

Never say, "Impossible."

Shigeo Shingo

We think that "impossible" is an attribute of a situation or circumstance. Not so long ago, people thought it was science fiction to travel to the moon and back. Now, we are heading to Mars. More recently, who would say that we would be having free video calls anywhere in the world, or have your entire body coded onto a microchip? Sure, the moment "impossible" was used we weren't traveling to the moon nor making video calls, free or not. For most of us it looked like it might always be impossible, but thankfully not everyone thinks that way

For some people just the remote possibility engages their imagination, their passion and energy. Were it not for such people we would still be just gazing at the moon and stuck with pigeon post.

"Possible" is a position we take — and so is "impossible." Some people would say it is impossible to improve on great things. For Toyota, people said it was possible to continue to improve on the Toyota Camry, one of the best cars on the market. In the Georgetown, Kentucky, plant they improve it at the rate of over 200,000 times every year — nearly 25 adopted improvements per person per year. Their "possible" stance sustains those year-after-year gains. Not so far away, the old Big Three automakers struggle to get two adopted improvements for every person working on the line. Today, Tesla is speeding past these giants at a tremendous pace.

We call "possible" a stance — a way of living one's life. For Lean leaders, "possible" is just the way it is.

What looks impossible to you and your colleagues? What, if it were possible, would bring significantly more value to your customers, your colleagues, and your company?

What is getting in your way of taking the "possible" stance? Will you sound crazy? People have said that before! Are you afraid you won't succeed? You've failed before. Do you need to see evidence? Many big breakthroughs were built on dreams.

"Possible" is the declaration for each of us to make in the face of something worthwhile. It is the only stance that will bring it to fruition.

Mission Possible Kata

What possibility will you stand for? Write it down. Share it with others. Yes, share it with others. Enroll them in what you say is possible. Ask them to expand on the possibility. Share it again and again and again, each time asking to expand the possibility. It's the only way to get on the Lean journey.

Make notes along the way of your thoughts, others' reactions and moods.

Hansei

What is it like taking a stance for possibility? What did you notice about your emotions? What did you hear from others? What are you doing for yourself to stay in that possibility? Finally, what action will you take to start realizing the possibility?

JOURNAL

Afterword

Hal asked me, before I had seen this book, to read it, step back and put it in a larger context. I accepted and then he sent me the book. I took a walk after reading the first few pages, came back and read it through twice. And then remembered a favorite quote but not its author: "We can see and feel the waste of material things. Awkward, inefficient, or ill directed movements of workers leaves nothing visible or tangible behind. Their appreciation calls for an act of memory, an effort of the imagination."[‡] Hold that thought.

The focus improvement in the construction industry prior to Lean Construction, was on motivation and training of the workforce. In the 1950's the application of the Critical Path Method opened a new route and Contracts changed. Subcontractors focused on their trade, often at the expense of others and the project. Partnering helped some, but many became cynical.

The Lean Construction movement began for me when Glenn Ballard asked a simple question: "How well does planning work." We quickly found that crews completed about 50% of their planned work each week. Work assignments failed most frequently for lack of logistics or the failure of coordination. A lot has happened since, as the principals and practices of Lean Construction developed. We read some books. We borrowed heavily from the examples, principles, and practices of *The Toyota Way*. Now comes the next step, one which requires us to become more mindful and observant.

Hal Macomber & Calayde Davey open a new path, take a different route establishing a step-by-step steady principle-based practice. My guess is you will first try to read the book through and make improvements as the opportunities pop up. That is exactly what I did for a few days....

Don't do that!

Rather, read each chapter as they come. Reflect, reconsider, write down your reflections and learning in the journal. Develop the step-by-step routine of following the *kata*, reflecting, journaling, and learning. I believe you will change what and how you remember things as you apply more carefully those acts of memory, mastery, and efforts of imagination.

— Gregory A. Howell, P.E.
Cofounder and past President of the
Lean Construction Institute

[‡] Fredrick Taylor, *"Principles of Scientific Management."* 1911

Special Thanks

We've had a lot of help in getting this book published. Thanks to all those who reviewed and commented on this work, making it far better than we could do alone.

To Fernando Flores and Chauncey Bell, two people who've been in my life since the late '80s. I can't convey all I learned from Fernando about the nature of human beings and our functioning in the world. Without that foundation, I could not have written this book, created the *katas*, and do the work I do for clients. Fernando's gift to the world of the language-action perspective is one of the great contributions of the late 20th century.

I learned to collaborate from Chauncey. Reflecting on my career, my best work, and certainly my best thinking happened in conversations and partnership with him. I am honored to have Chauncey write the Forward.

To my colleagues at Lean Project Consulting who have provided me with challenging work and opportunities for collaboration and innovation. Cheri Phelps for help with the book title, Rebecca Snelling for seeing that Lean leaders will find their own way through the book, Christine Slivon for careful criticism and guidance on the *katas* and Greg Howell for inspiring me to write the book and for the Afterward.

To Calayde, my collaborator, editor, and illustrator extraordinaire for her determination, discipline, and support to bring this book to completion and make it beautiful.

And to my family, who never complained when I stole an hour or two almost every day for a few months writing the book. They know I'll do it again!

— Hal Macomber

For all the wonderfully imaginative friends and neighbors in the River Market, Kansas City, and the family and friends from South Africa, Spain, and New Zealand cheering us on. This book is a result of pure camaraderie, good humor, and fanciful learning. Thank you so much for keeping our joy and motivation high during this time — without you, we would be boring.

— Calayde Davey

Your

TOOLKIT

What do you want to learn today?

ON MOODS

We repeatedly refer to moods, starting with the introductions and throughout the *hanseis*. Moods are particularly important for successful learning. One commonsense understanding is that moods and emotions are the same. We are using the words differently. In large part, emotions are situational responses. While watching a movie, a particular scene can trigger an emotional response on a range from mad to sad or happy to glad. The response is transitory. We laugh or cry and then we stop.

While moods can also be situational, they tend to linger and we can bring them into the situation. One can go into the situation with a predisposition about what it will be like. For instance, one might bring a mood of boredom to a party. The mood colors what is possible at the party. While other attendees might be engaged and cheerful, the person bringing a mood of boredom may never get engaged and leave the party in the same mood.

Some moods are pervasive. You've heard people described as "ever the optimist" or "always a pessimist." This characterization or assessment we might call a "walking around" mood — the person brings the mood without regard or response to the situation at hand.

Moods can choose us *and* we can choose our moods. Some people get anxious at the thought of taking a test even when they know the subject and are well-prepared. They "fall" into that mood. Alternatively, the knowledgeable and well-prepared person could choose to bring confidence to her test-taking.

One way to recognize one's own mood is to observe or listen to the incessant silent self-talk — that "little voice" in your head. The anxious person may be saying, "This won't work out for me. I'll forget the answers to the questions. I'll run out of time." We can think of that as giving in to the mood. Alternatively, an individual who chooses or produces the mood of confidence is saying, "I've got this — it is just as I prepared" or "Oops! I missed that one, but will get the rest." These two people are equally prepared but they perform differently based on their mood.

You can recognize others' moods in a similar way by noticing the conversation they are in. "Normal" people don't say their self-talk out loud. Instead, we give clues to our disposition or attitude. When learning something new, one person might say, "That looks difficult," and then pass on trying the task at all. While another person says, "I wonder how long it will take me to learn that?" and then tries. The first person might be in a mood of trepidation or worry while the second person is in the mood of wonder and determination.

Moods arise out of the past and project to the future. We've referred to moods as (pre)dispositions, attitudes, and conversations. In all cases the mood is grounded in some "story" about a past experience coupled with an anticipation about the future. The anxious test-taker likely had an experience that didn't go well. The anxious mood arises in the conversation that the performance will repeat the next time around. Notice that the person is making an assessment that the past experience will continue to the future. This could be grounded — the situations could be nearly identical — or not grounded — the situations are not at all the same. Moods pervade when we don't notice the assessment we are making and fail to examine the grounding.

Beware: moods are contagious! As you learn to become a Lean leader, you will learn faster if you take responsibility for your moods and the moods of the people with whom you interact. You are just as likely to "catch" the mood of those around you as they are to "catch" your mood. When you bring a mood of confidence to a situation grounded in the preparation that you've made, then others will have confidence in you and in their participation with you. Alternatively, you might "catch" their uncertainty to experiment out of fear that results won't be positive. "We can't try that!" they say, and it becomes your mood as well.

Concerns are in the background of all moods. By "concern" we mean some unaddressed and usually pervasive matter or interest that we generally care for. Human beings in the western world today generally share concerns for their well-being and the well-being of others. We have concerns for money or wealth, body or our health, family, friendships, spirituality, play, education, career, the world, and our dignity.[25] Our moods, attitudes, and predispositions associate with how we are taking care of our concerns and then project how we will continue to do so.

A concern for "looking good" or "being right" is fundamentally about our dignity and our place in our social network. Fixating on either looking good or being right gets in the way of successfully taking action, which inevitably produces just the opposite result of what we are concerned about! The anxious test-taker creates the conditions for not doing well.

We claim that to succeed in developing yourself as a Lean leader you must be an open learner. Specifically, you must embrace that you will make mistakes in a setting that others will observe and your concerns for dignity, career, work, and associations with your network will not be jeopardized in the process. Further, the repeated practice of open learning will produce the esteem of others, their support, and participation in your success. While you might work in an environment where that is a foreign concept, taking the step of learning in the open will interrupt the "way things are around here." You will create that condition when you bring the moods of Wonder (where might this take me (us))? Humor (oops, I did it again!), and Determination (I'll take another go).

Look for the above moods as you practice your *katas*. Once you notice your mood, you're on your way to making it work for you.

Supportive moods	Unsupportive moods
wonder	confusion
perplexity	resignation
serenity/acceptance	frustration
patience	arrogance
ambition	impatience
resolution	boredom
confidence	fear/anxiety
trust	overwhelm
	lack of confidence
	distrust

This list of moods comes from Gloria Flores' book, pages 20 and 25, respectively.

For more background on moods see:

Conversations for Action and Collected Essays, by Fernando Flores, (7) Managing Moods and (11) *Recurrent Domains of Human Concerns.* 2012

Learning to Learn and the Navigation of Moods: The Meta-Skill for the Acquisition of Skills, by Gloria Flores. 2016

A3 THINKING AND LEARNING

A3 is the international designation for paper about 11 x 17 inches. Toyota adopted the approach of presenting their reports concisely in a rather standard way to tell the story of how a goal is being pursued or a problem is being solved.

A3s are "hot" in the Lean space. You'll hear managers say, "Write me an A3 on that." "Capture the problem we solved on an A3." "Make an A3 for the client." None of these requests represent the intent of A3 thinking and learning. The A3 is an artifact, a report, that is *used throughout* the goal-seeking or problem-solving process. We use the A3 thinking framework to keep our attention on learning throughout goal-seeking and problem-solving. At the conclusion, the A3 report is a concise *story* of what a group learned and accomplished.

A3 thinking is based on the *Plan → Do → Study → Act* learning cycle created by Dr. Shewhart, widely taught by Dr. W. Edwards Deming, and became famous when Toyota communicated it as the basis of the Toyota Business Process. For Toyota, A3 learning fits with it's purpose, their reason for being, to develop human potential.

There are two roles when working with an A3 report: the report writer and the report reviewer. The writer is often the champion of the goal-seeking or problem-solving process. That person is working with others who have the interests and expertise to reach a successful conclusion. The reviewer acts as a mentor or coach to the writer. The reviewer's attention is on developing the writer's critical thinking skills and socio-political skills to bring actions through to implementation. Notice the difference between this and the prior requests.

This is not a book on succeeding with A3 thinking and learning. You can find many good sources with good examples. Here are four:

- *Managing to Learn,* by John Shook
- *Getting the Right Things Done,* by Pascal Dennis
- *Understanding A3 Thinking,* by Durward K. Sobek and Art Smalley
- *A3 Problem Solving: Applying Lean Thinking,* by Jamie Flinchbaugh

ADVANCED OHNO CIRCLE
30 MINUTES | 30 WASTES | 30 DAYS

Taiichi Ohno famously would draw a chalk circle on the factory floor and insist (invite) someone stand there for quite some time making observations of waste. While it might appear to be a kind of punishment, Ohno was training people to find waste. Usually, once we see waste, we'll know what to do about it.

This advanced exercise is inspired by the *Kaizen Exercise: Stand in the Circle,*[26] a blog post by Jon Miller in Gemba Panta Rei. Jon says to stand in a work area for 30 minutes looking for 30 wastes. Once 30 have been recorded or when 30 minutes have elapsed, the viewer picks one waste to eliminate with the help of the person who was observed involved with the waste.

In the next 30 minutes the two people find the root cause and implement countermeasures.

Eliminating the waste might not be straightforward. Remember, we want to eliminate wastes at the root of the problem. You may need to engage in a Five Why, Good Five Why, or value stream mapping to identify the source of the waste.

Install a countermeasure. Make a record of the improvement activity capturing: what problem did we have? What change did we make? How did it get better? Take before and after photos if appropriate.

Use the next 30 days to tackle the balance of your list.

FIVE WHYS
TRADITIONAL

Toyota says that "5 Ws = 1 H." Most people understand that to mean who, what, where, when and why; we then add how. But that is not what Toyota means. Toyota, specifically Dr. Shingo, understands that *"we can discover the true causes of things by asking why, why, why, why, and why over and over again,"* [11] Shingo goes on to point out that this process reveals how goals and means trade places with each answer to why. As a result, we get to the root cause(s) of the problem avoiding the error of improving at superficial levels.

One good example of the 5 Why process comes from *The Toyota Way.*

	Level of Problem	Corresponding Level of Countermeasure
	There is a puddle of oil on the shop floor	Clean up the oil
Why?	Because the machine is leaking oil	Fix the machine
Why?	Because the gasket has deteriorated	Replace the gasket
Why?	Because we bought gaskets made of inferior material	Change gasket specifications
Why?	Because we got a good deal (price) on those gaskets	Change purchasing policies
Why?	Because the purchasing agent gets evaluated on short-term cost savings	Change the evaluation policy for purchasing agents

GOOD 5-WHY — BRANCHING PROCESS

The concept of a *Good Five Why*™ came from a two-day visit to the Toyota Georgetown main plant organized by Norman Bodek. One of our meetings was with Gary Convis, President of Toyota Motors Manufacturing North America. During the conversation one of our participants asked Gary a question about the importance of advanced problem-solving approaches. Gary replied that Toyota couldn't make the progress they do without having some people who are competent using advanced problem-solving tools. He added that the vast majority of improvements made across the company — at least 80% — started and finished with what he called "a good five why."

That statement gnawed at Hal for over a year. He couldn't figure out how the five why linear process could produce so many improvements. Our experience was that you could get one or maybe two improvements from a five why. That would mean Toyota was conducting more than a million annually. That didn't seem possible.

Hal found the clue to Gary's statement in *The Toyota Way Fieldbook*.[27] Five whys are not simple linear problem-cause-problem statements. The diagrams showed two answers at the 5th why. Five whys branched. This is what Gary meant by a "good five why." When branching is involved you'll get 10 - 20 improvements instead of one or two improvements. That changed the math on how many five whys Toyota does in a year.

Here's the *Good 5-Why*™ protocol:

- What is the immediate or observed problem?
- What countermeasure can you take?
- Why did that variance occur?
- What other plausible answers are there for why the variance occurred?
- What countermeasures can you take for each of those causes?
- For each of those causes, why did that variance occur?
- What other plausible answers are there?
- What countermeasures can you take for those causes?

And so on…

The *Good Five Why*™ diagram of problem - causes - problems (notice plurals) looks like the branching of a tree.

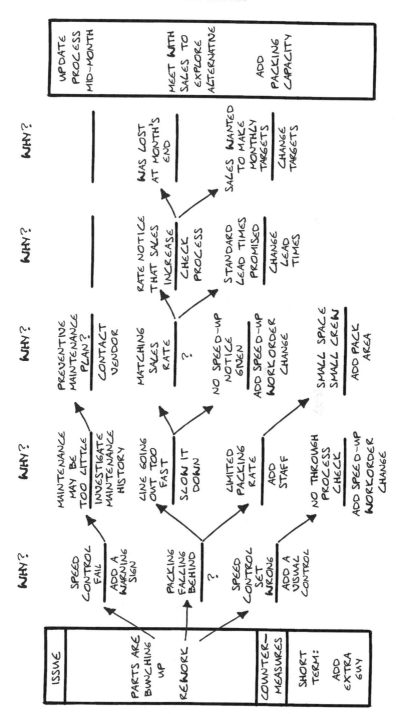

FISHBONE DIAGRAM

Dr. Kaoru Ishikawa is credited with inventing the process for diagrammatically examining causes and their effects in a whole systems way. The early examples were production related. They explored the four Ms: man, machine, methods and materials. Dr. Ishikawa recognized that problems or variances (differences from expectations) were the result of a number of possible causes often coming together simultaneously. For instance, a defect appears when there may be some irregularity in the machine that is coupled with how the operator is using the machine.

Later, three other Ms were added: management, metrics (measurements), and milieu (environment).

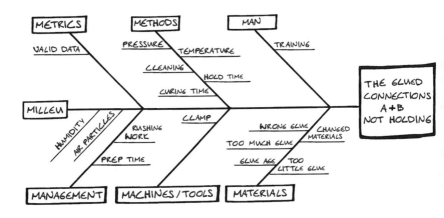

GLOSSARY

8th Waste

Providing the customer something that he or she doesn't value. Blister packaging comes to mind.

Making do with what you have at hand often results in some aspect of the product or service that doesn't meet customer expectations. This requires normally uncalled for effort, or rework. Professor Lauri Koskela first distinguished this waste.[28]

The untapped potential of people. One prominent way this arises is when the people doing the work — those that have the best knowledge of the status quo — are not engaged in the improvement of the work.

first-run study

While Lean has us consider all work as experiments from which we can learn, the first-run study is a planned experiment conducted the first time that a group performs an operation. These experiments are usually videoed so the performers can evaluate their performance. First-run studies follow the *PDSA* framework for learning. Teams usually take multiple *PDSA* passes to explore alternative approaches and refine their process.

flow

Flow is the uninterrupted accumulation of value from the customer's perspective. *Flow* is impeded or interrupted in a number of ways including bottlenecks, variation, large lots, work not being ready, and queues. *Flow* is visible in physical production settings like assembly lines, kitchens, art projects, and construction. *Flow* is invisible in the "production" of knowledge work. And, knowledge work is interrupted in the same five ways as physical work. The Kanban Method is routinely adopted for professional services work to make *flow* and *flow* interruptions visible.

It's helpful to look at *flow* from at least two perspectives: cycle time — from the time production activities are prepared through the completion of the value-added work, and overall lead time — from customer order to customer receipt. The actions one takes are usually different on either side of the cycle time.

Variation has a large impact on system performance, which degrades exponentially as demand approaches system capacity. The most familiar example of this is the highway that is speedy during the midday, yet is stop-and-go during rush hour.

You can make a quick improvement to flow by limiting work-in-process. The more WIP you have, the more items are not being worked on. Cut the WIP and you'll cut the items not being worked on. You'll also shorten the time for all the work.

flow efficiency

This is a measure of how much of the duration is value-added time, calculated as VAT/cycle time and expressed as a percent.

gemba

the place of the real work — the value-adding work for the customer.

genchi genbutsu

go to see for yourself at *gemba*

hoshin kanri

also known as "policy deployment." This is a strategy development and implementation process for a company or business unit. The intent is to identify one to three key challenges that apply broadly within the firm for a medium time horizon — two to three years.

Hoshin kanri is conducted from the top-down and bottom-up. "Top" is meant to be a group that is looking at the firm from the market back into the company. This view, as Taiichi Ohno says, *the source of information is always the customer.* The group investigates pervasive customer concerns such as satisfaction, fitness for purpose, maintenance, pricing, etc. The findings are then cascaded down the organization to explore the concerns. The process then returns up the organization with specific direction and plans to the original group.

Traditionally, firms begin at senior management working down to those working in the value stream. Enlightened firms start the process with a cross-section of the organization. Hal remembers visiting a company in Japan in the 1980s where they stated their process began by interviewing the most recent college hires. They asked the question, "What kind of company do you want to work for when you retire?"

Ohno's 7 Wastes

Overproduction — producing anything that hasn't been sold or isn't being used immediately. This includes making product earlier than needed. You can overproduce estimates, drawings, and documents just as you can overproduce parts. Doing something earlier than needed takes on the risk that it will need to be done over or corrected.

Waiting — we incur waste when people are waiting for work and when work is waiting for processing. In the second case *flow efficiency* decreases when a *flow unit* is waiting for processing. Batch production insures that all but the one *flow unit* in processing will be waiting.

Unnecessary transportation — anytime we are moving material around without beginning the next processing step, the transportation is unnecessary. Dr. Shingo called transportation a crime! *Flow efficiency falls* when transport occurs and the *flow unit* doesn't move to the next step.

Over-processing — this occurs when we fail to understand how our action contributes to the desired outcome. Good example: trying to spit-shine a canvas sneaker. It's not possible *and* trying will result in rework to remove the spit!

Excess Inventory — While Engineer Ohno called inventory a waste, he also found temporary good uses for inventory. Having some extra stock on hand prior to a forecast snow storm can keep the plant busy. Asking an engineer to do some work earlier than needed (overproducing) so she can be available later for other work does increase the risk of reworking the early work but increases her ability to deal with other demands. The key here is recognizing what is excess while examining risks.

Unnecessary movement — This waste is about the person performing work. Reaching, sorting, leaving your workspace to retrieve something, and walking are all not adding value and might be necessary. The opportunity is to see that necessary work as temporary, until you improve it.

Defects — Corrective action is required with defects, but defects imply more waste than that. If you are making defects, then you might put inspection in place to find the defects. Inspecting 100 items to find 3 defects is wasted action on 97 items. Fail-safing (*poka yoke*) and through-process inspection reduce or eliminate errors minimizing this waste.

PDSA

Plan → *Do* → *Study* → *Act* was first introduced by Dr. Shewhart as *Plan* → *Do* → *Check* → *Act*. Dr. W. Edwards Deming changed "check" to "study" to emphasize that we want to be learning at every possible time. "Check" has come to be understood as validate the hypothesis or verify one's results. Lean leaders understand the importance of tightly coupling learning with action. "Study" is closer to Dr. Deming's intent and so we use it here.

Think of this process as the scientific method for everyday use. The "plan" portion is the hypothesis or expectation. It's only when we act with expectations that we can explicitly identify variances. No expectation, no variance, no learning, no improvement. Another way to think of *PDSA* is as a mental model for experimentation for all operations and actions. The brilliance of adopting *PDSA* for your organization or project is that all work becomes the experiments needed to realize continuous improvement.

Plus | Delta

This a quick three to five minute improvement process for eliciting group assessments on a recent meeting or activity. Conduct a *Plus|Delta* at the conclusion of any activity that lasts about 30 minutes and up to two hours. You ask the group to share what produced value (plus) for them personally and what they request or propose to do differently (delta) in any follow-on activity. Results of the conversation are captured on a chart.

The next time the group convenes, the group reviews the most recent plus | deltas for the sake of building on the pluses and addressing one or more of the deltas. Conducting *Plus|Deltas* frequently builds the participants' confidence with making in-the-moment assessments. This builds shared responsibility for the outcome of any group process.

poka yoke

This translates loosely as "fail-safing." Poka yoke devices keep the performer of an operation from making or passing along defects. They range from approaches that keep the worker safe to those that ensure the safety of the customer. Everyday examples: fuel handles at filling stations that don't allow you to put the wrong fuel in your tank; electrical outlets that don't allow you to plug in the wrong kind of devices; and the pop-through button on an outdoor table umbrella that ensures the pole is secure. Do an image search on the web for more examples.

Quick 'n Easy Kaizen

QnEK is everyday small improvements initiated and usually implemented by the person doing the work. There are some minimum conditions for these *QnEK*: (1) one only has permission to improve one's own job; (2) the improvement must be recorded answering the questions, What problem did I have? What change did I make? How did it get better? (3) one must immediately inform one's supervisor presenting the short report. Many situations call for more than that, particularly when life safety issues are involved.

Good performance with everyday *QnEK* is two adopted improvements per person per month for every employee. Seem like a stretch? Toyota gets about one per week. Subaru gets about two per week. Fastcap gets one each day from every person. Start with two!

Study-Action Teams™

These are generally reading-based discussion groups that are organized to pursue some large objective or challenge that the group needs to learn about before they set out in pursuit of the challenge. Readings are organized so the group can discuss in one-hour blocks. The intent is to use the challenge as the context for the reading. Discussions primarily focus on what the author wants the reader to learn. Each discussion concludes with an exploration of how those key learnings apply to the challenge and what actions might be possible. The team conducts a planning session at the conclusion of the series of discussions. Hal Macomber created the *Study-Action Team* format in the 1980's. SAT's are in wide use in the design and construction industry.

See Study-Action Teams, *Opening Minds for Organizational Change*, by Christine Slivon and Hal Macomber, www.leanproject.com/access-whitepapers/

Two Great Wastes

The origin of *Two Great Wastes* was a conversation Hal overheard following a weekly job-site foreman's meeting. There were a few challenges discussed at the meeting. Few people had anything to say. The superintendent (the job-site leader) did a lot of talking and note-taking, all without picking his head up to look at the participants in the meeting. On the platform outside the job-site trailer two foremen commented, "The superintendent never listens to us. It's why we gave up talking."

Not speaking and not listening are the two great wastes. You can trace many other wastes to someone with an answer who doesn't share it or someone doesn't listen to an answer when it's spoken. Pay attention at meetings, in ad hoc conversations, and when there is a problem at hand. Are you listening? Do you have something to offer but you are not speaking? Can you recognize either of those conditions in others? You will avoid a lot of waste if you look for the Two Great Wastes.

See *The Two Great Wastes in Organizations*, by Hal Macomber and Gregory Howell. IGLC-12. Helsinkor, Denmark 2004. http://iglc. net/Papers/Details/303

REFERENCES

1. **Edison, Thomas A.** "From the Laboratory of Thomas A. Edison," *Journal of the Franklin Institute* 179, no. 6 (1915): 720.

2. **Koskela, Lauri.** "Making-Do — the Eighth Category of Waste," 2004. http://eprints.hud.ac.uk/26019.

3. **Shingo, Shigeo.** *Zero Quality Control: Source Inspection and the Poka-Yoke System.* CRC Press, 1986.

4. **Spears, Stephen J.** *The High-Velocity Edge: How Market Leaders Leverage Operational Excellence to Beat the Competition.* Second Edition. McGraw-Hill Education, 2010.

5. **Fishman, Charles.** "No Satisfaction at Toyota." *Fast Company.* Fast Company, December 1, 2006. https://www.fastcompany.com/58345/no-satisfaction-toyota.

6. **Psarouthakis, John.** *Better Makes Us Best.* Productivity Press, 1989.

7. **Inc Global Market Insights**, "Material Handling Equipment Market Worth over $190bn by 2024" (Global Market Insights, Inc., April 13, 2017), https://www.gminsights.com/pressrelease/material-handling-equipment-market?utm_source=globenewswire.com&utm_medium=referral&utm_campaign=Paid_Globnewswire.

8. **Ford, Henry.** *Today and Tomorrow. Special Edition of Ford's 1926 Classic.* Productivity Press, Cambridge, Mass, 1988.

9. **Ohno, Taiichi.** *Toyota Production System: Beyond Large-Scale Production.* CRC Press, 1988.

10. **Deming, W. Edwards.** *Out of the Crisis.* The MIT Press, 1982.

11. **Liker, Jeffrey K.** *The Toyota Way: 14 Management Principles from the World's Greatest Manufacturer.* McGraw-Hill, 2004.

12. **KPMG.** "Global Automotive Executive Survey 2017." KPMG, 2017. https://assets.kpmg.com/content/dam/kpmg/xx/pdf/2017/01/global-automotive-executive-survey-2017.pdf.

13. **Anderson, David J.** "Kanban's 3 Agendas." http://www.djaa.com/kanbans-3-agendas. referenced July 16, 2017

14. **Modig, Niklas and Ahlstrom, Par.** *This Is Lean.* (11) Rheologica Publishing, 2012

15. **Gawande, Atul.** *The Checklist Manifesto: How to Get Things Right.* Metropolitan Books, 2009.

16. **Womack, James P., and Daniel T. Jones.** *Lean Thinking Banish Waster and Create Wealth In Your Corporation.* Simon & Schuster Publishers, New York, New York, USA, 1996.

17. **Miller, Jon.** "Give Me 60 Minutes and I'll Give You a Lean Transformation." Http://blog.gembaacademy.com/, March 5, 2007. http://blog.gembaacademy.com/2007/03/05/give_me_60_minutes_and_ill_giv/.

18. **Luft, J., and Ingham, H.** "The Johari Window." Human Relations Training News 5, no. 1 (1961): 6–7.

19. **The Aspen Institute.** "The Aspen Institute." Accessed 2017. https://www.aspeninstitute.org/.

20. **TED.** "TED." Https://www.ted.com/about/programs-Initiatives, n.d. Accessed 2017.

21. **Hawken, P., Lovins A.B., and Lovins. L. H.** *Natural Capitalism: The Next Industrial Revolution.* Routledge, 2013.

22. **TWI Institute.** "On-the-Job Instruction." TWI Institute, January 1985. doi:10.1080/00185868.1985.9948400.

23. **Macomber, Hal, & Howell, Gregory.** 2004, 'The Two Great Wastes in Organizations' In:, Bertelsen, S. & Formoso, C.T., 12th Annual Conference of the International Group for Lean Construction. Helsingør, Denmark, 3-5 Aug 2004.

24. **Shingo, Shigeo.** *Key Strategies for Plant Improvement.* Taylor & Francis, 1987.

25. **Flores, Fernando,** "Conversations for Action and Collected Essays. (11), Pgs 107, 108. 2012.

26. http://blog.gembaacademy.com/2009/03/23/kaizen_exercise_stand_in_the_circle/

27. **Liker, Jeffrey K. and Meiers, David.** *The Toyota Way Fieldbook.* In Chapter 15, Page 343-344, figures 15-1 and 15-2.

28. **Koskela, L. J.** "Making do - the eighth category of waste." *12th Annual Conference of the International Group for Lean Construction,* 3-5 August 2004, Helsingor, Denmark. https://usir.salford.ac.uk/9386/

29. **Akers, Paul.** *Two Second Lean - 3rd Edition.* BookBaby, 2016.

QUOTES

PART I

1. **Give new ideas a chance.** - Ohno, Taiichi. Workplace Management, Productivity Press, 1988.(4) p.13.

2. **Confirm failure with your own eyes.** - Ohno, Taiichi. *Workplace Management*, Productivity Press, 1988.(4) p.12.

3. **Take action immediately if a defect is detected.** - Shingo, Shigeo. *Kaizen and The Art of Creative Thinking.* Enna Products Corporation, 2007. (8) p.48.

4. **Make only what you can sell.** - Ohno, Taiichi. *Workplace Management*, Productivity Press, 1988. (8) p.30.

5. **Don't be afraid of lost opportunities.** - Ohno, Taiichi. *Workplace Management*, Productivity Press, 1988.(7) p.25

6. **Dissatisfaction is the 'mother' of improvement.** - Shingo, Shigeo. *Non-Stock Production: The Shingo System of Continuous Improvement.* CRC Press, 1988. (3) p.18.

7. **People who are satisfied with the way things are can never achieve improvement of progress.** - Shingo, Shigeo. *The Sayings of Shigeo Shingo,* 1987. (3) p.17.

8. **Never accept the status quo.** - Shingo, Shigeo. *The Sayings of Shigeo Shingo,* 1987. (3) p.17.

PART II

9. **Transportation is a crime.** - Shingo, Shigeo. *Kaizen and The Art of Creative Thinking.* Enna Products Corporation, 2007. p.391.

10. **The source of information is always the customer.** - Ohno, Taiichi, and Setsuo Mito. *Just-in-Time for Today and Tomorrow.* Productivity Press, 1988.(1) p.10

11. **Wasted motion is not work.** - Ohno, Taiichi. *Workplace Management*, Productivity Press, 1988.(11) p.41

12. **Small minds want more space.** - Shingo, Shigeo. *The Sayings of Shigeo Shingo,* 1987. (6) p.87

13. **If you don't know why defects are occurring, make some defects.** - Shingo, Shigeo. *The Sayings of Shigeo Shingo,* 1987. (7) p.105.

14. **We must always grasp the real facts – i.e., what is – rather than what ought to be.** - Shingo, Shigeo. *The Sayings of Shigeo Shingo,* 1987. (4) p.28.

15. **We must dig up the real cause by asking why, why, why, why, why.** - Ohno, Taiichi. *Toyota production system: beyond large-scale production.* CRC Press, 1988.(glossary) p.127.

16. **The same as yesterday isn't good enough.** - Shingo, Shigeo. *The Sayings of Shigeo Shingo,* 1987. (8) p.117.

PART III

17. **Our invariable response to, "It can't be done" is, "Do it!"** – Ford, Henry. *Today and Tomorrow. Special Edition of Ford's 1926 Classic.* Productivity Press, Cambridge, Mass, 1988. (5) p.53.

18. **Illusions can easily turn into conventional wisdom.** - Ohno, Taiichi. *Workplace Management,* Productivity Press, 1988.(5) p.17

19. **Distinguish between movement and work to cultivate the ability to find waste.** - Ohno, Taiichi. *Workplace Management,* Productivity Press, 1988.(11) p.44.

20. **The greatest waste is the waste we don't see.** - Shingo, Shigeo. *The Sayings of Shigeo Shingo,* 1987. (3) p.19.

21. **Before anything else, give it a try.** - Shingo, Shigeo. *The Sayings of Shigeo Shingo,* 1987. (8) p.107.

22. **We must exhaustively pursue our true objectives – the abstract objects lying beyond what is visible.** - Shingo, Shigeo. *The Sayings of Shigeo Shingo,* 1987. (2) p.14.

23. **Rationalize your operation when business is booming.** - Ohno, Taiichi. *Workplace Management,* Productivity Press, 1988.(14) p.55.

24. **The medicine won't work unless you take it.** - Shingo, Shigeo. *The Sayings of Shigeo Shingo,* 1987. (10) p.160.

PART IV

25. **We will not be able to blaze new trails unless we boldly turn our thinking processes upside down, and unless everyone participates in that revolution.** - Ohno, Taiichi. *Workplace Management*, Productivity Press, 1988.(5) p.18.

26. **We use checklists so not to forget that we have forgotten.** - Shingo, Shigeo. *The Sayings of Shigeo Shingo*, 1987. (2) p.14.

27. **Find problems where you think none exist.** - Shingo, Shigeo. *The Sayings of Shigeo Shingo*, 1987. (3) p.18.

28. **Everyone confuses motion with work.** - Ohno, Taiichi. *Workplace Management*, Productivity Press, 1988.(11) p.43.

29. **Usually mass production raises costs.** - Ohno, Taiichi. *Workplace Management* (10) p.38

30. **The best way to clean something is to make sure it doesn't get dirty in the first place.** - Shingo, Shigeo. *The Sayings of Shigeo Shingo*, 1987. (7) p.100.

31. **Stand on the production floor all day and watch – eventually you will discover what has to be done.** - Ohno, Taiichi. *Toyota production system: beyond large-scale production.* CRC Press, 1988.(4) p.78

32. **All our knowledge and understanding won't get us anywhere unless we are able to act on it.** - Shingo, Shigeo. *The Sayings of Shigeo Shingo,*(2) p.15.

PART V

33. **If we don't understand what it is that we don't understand, we have no idea what to do about it.** - Shingo, Shigeo. *The Sayings of Shigeo Shingo*, 1987. (4) p.29.

34. **"Know-how" alone isn't enough! You need "know-why!"** - Shingo, Shigeo. *The Sayings of Shigeo Shingo*, 1987. (5) p.68.

35. **Understanding alone isn't enough to get people moving.** - Shingo, Shigeo. *The Sayings of Shigeo Shingo*, 1987. (9) p.129.

36. **We act on what we think is true. Don't act on assumptions.** - Shingo, Shigeo. *The Sayings of Shigeo Shingo,* 1987. (10) p.158.

37. **Find waste!** - Shingo, Shigeo. *Non-Stock Production: The Shingo System of Continuous Improvement.* CRC Press, 1988. (3) p.71.

38. **"Eliminate waste!" is a nonsensical slogan.** - Shingo, Shigeo. *The Sayings of Shigeo Shingo,* 1987. (10) p.19.

39. **When carrying out improvements, you will only be truly effective when you first set your objectives and then head straight for them.** - Shingo, Shigeo. *The Sayings of Shigeo Shingo,* 1987. (5) p.53

40. **Never say, "Impossible."** - Shingo, Shigeo. *The Sayings of Shigeo Shingo,* 1987. (10) p.158.

HAL MACOMBER   CALAYDE DAVEY

Hal did his first production system project in the summer of 1974 in the butcher department of a supermarket. He followed that with a two-year stint in the operations research department of the Bank of Boston in 1976 - 1978. Hal was selected to study quality and just-in-time production in Japan in the mid 1980's. That began the formal introduction to Lean which spanned numerous industries and professions. Along the way, Hal was introduced to the work of Fernando Flores -- first the study of the language-action perspective, then ontological redesign. Those bodies of knowledge coupled to Lean allowed him and his collaborators to make very large scale organizational interventions.

Hal and his wife Rita live in the White Mountains of New Hampshire among many good friends

Calayde studied her masters in architecture in South Africa, and with the help of a Fulbright Scholarship, obtained a PhD in Environmental Planning, Economics, and Urban Development at Kansas State University. In her last few years in the U.S. she worked on a Lean Integrated Project Delivery (IPD) project in the roles of Lean production engineering and building information modeling. Calayde has a life-long love of performing chamber and orchestral music with her friends, and a recent affair with rock climbing. And as you can see from her illustrations, she also has a life-long dedication to curiosity, which is inspired by the shared trails and tribulations of a wonderful community of colleagues, friends, and family.

Calayde has returned to her home country of South Africa for the time being.

63182831R00137

Made in the USA
Middletown, DE
30 January 2018